CATAKISM

Bow to the Meow

CATAKISM

Bow to the Meow

A HUMOROUS PURR-SPECTIVE ON
HUMANKIND'S OBSESSION WITH CATS

JEFF LAZARUS

Skyhorse Publishing

Skyhorse Publishing books may be purchased in bulk at special discounts for sales promotion, corporate gifts, fund-raising, or educational purposes. Special editions can also be created to specifications. For details, contact the Special Sales Department, Skyhorse Publishing, 307 West 36th Street, 11th Floor, New York, NY 10018 or info@skyhorsepublishing.com.

Skyhorse® and Skyhorse Publishing® are registered trademarks of Skyhorse Publishing, Inc.®, a Delaware corporation.

Visit our website at www.skyhorsepublishing.com.

10 9 8 7 6 5 4 3 2 1

Library of Congress Cataloging-in-Publication Data is available on file.

Cover design by Peter Green Design and Jeff Lazarus
Cover images: Adobe Stock
Interior images: iStockphoto.com

Print ISBN: 978-1-5107-2645-1
Ebook ISBN: 978-1-5107-2647-5

Printed in China

Let us begin with a prayer . . .

We, the Crazy Cat People, do solemnly vow to praise and pamper all purring beings.

We pledge to hold Thee, Cat, in higher regard than jobs, property, and sanity.

We promise never to refer to You as "that foot-high demon that lacerates my flesh and turns my flowerpot into a litter box," but only as "my fur angel."

We vow to shower You with toys, gadgets, gourmet treats, and luxury furniture—and we pray that You accept our gifts and do not pee on them.

We beg to be worthy of Your good graces and to never earn the Glare of Damnation.

And should we ever commit the sin of laughing at you for getting your head stuck in the tuna can, we will humbly ask for forgiveness.

We are, after all, lowly humans, and Thou art the Divine Feline.

Amen.

Cat·a·kis·m

noun

1. *The deep and reverent belief in Cat as master, guru, mentor, sage, and ridiculous ball of cuteness.*
2. *The devotional beliefs and rituals practiced by Catakists.*

Bow to the Meow

This doctrine is for practicing Catakists the world over. Are you among the faithful?

- 🐾 Do you refer to your cat's birthday as its Incarnation Anniversary?
- 🐾 Have you given serious thought to changing your Last Will and Testament to make Bootsy your prime beneficiary?
- 🐾 When your cat repeatedly perforates your thighs with its needle-sharp claws as part of its nightly lap dance, do you refer to this as "giving me a blessing," rather than "giving me a Guantanamo"?

If you answered yes to one or more of the above, welcome to the litter. These pages are dedicated to a simple premise: that humankind's obsession with kitties rises to the level of near worship and meets the criteria of a formal belief system. Catakism may not qualify for a tax exemption (yet), but its believers fanatically devote 78 percent (92 percent on the weekends) of their waking hours to praising their cats, shopping for their cats, stroking their cats, and conversing with their cats in high-pitched voices.

Name another belief system that inspires such dedicated and tireless purr-suit. Behold, the Nine Books of Catakism . . .

TABLE OF CONTENTS

THE BOOK OF WHISKERS

As whiskers are a cat's guide in life, the Book of Whiskers is the guide to the belief system known as Catakism.

I. The Belief in Cat

Human beings have a powerful need to *believe*, to throw themselves at the feet of something greater than they are. To worship. To adore. To make offerings and sacrifices to. To blame for not being happier, prettier, or more successful.

Throughout history, that "something greater than they are" has taken the form of volcanoes, trees, cows, stars, planets, elephants with eight arms, pharaohs, kings, totem poles, airplanes, giant phalluses, sci-fi novelists named Ron, money, and pretty much anything else not found stuck to the bottom of a shoe. Let's just say there's been a lot of trial and error on humanity's part.

But, over time, man's need to express devotion has crystallized into some deep and lasting belief systems. These belief systems have become the great isms and ologies of the world: Buddhism, Catholicism, Judaism, Hinduism; Astrology, Numerology, Dogtology, Scientology, mixology. Okay, the term "great" might not apply equally across the board here, but you get the point. There are well-known and named belief systems that are practiced by millions, even billions, of humans across the globe.

There are also unofficial beliefs that are practiced with uniform dedication by all of humankind, but they do not rise to the level of a formal religion. These include: If You Yell at Inanimate Objects Loudly Enough They Will Hear You and Obey; When You Check Your Teeth for Spinach in a Window Reflection, the Person on the Other Side of the Glass Can't See You; and Googling Yourself on a Daily Basis Is the Secret to Eternal Happiness.

Finally, there are deep belief systems that are practiced worldwide with the rabid devotion of a true religion, but they have not yet received an official name . . . until now. Catakism is the greatest of such belief systems.

Over the millennia, mankind's love of cats has risen from the simple human-to-pet relationship we enjoy with goldfish, hamsters, and parakeets to something much, *much* more. Kitties live in our hearts in a way we typically reserve for objects of true religious devotion.

What Is Catakism?

Catakism, in short, is mankind's unending and near-fanatical devotion to Cat. A Catakist does not consider a cat a *pet*, but rather a minor deity.

Scratch that (pun intended): major deity.

Catakism is more than the mere love or "ownership" (Seriously? Ownership?) of cats. Catakism is the belief that felines are elevated beings worthy of mankind's near-religious reverence and devotion. Is *worship* too strong a word for what Catakists do toward cats? Is "brisk" too strong a word for the temperature on Pluto?

Humanity has slowly been converting to Catakism for millennia, but now the conversion rate has reached fever pitch. Don't believe Catakism is among the major belief systems on Earth? Go on the Internet. Turn on your TV. Open a magazine. What do you see? Any questions?

The prevalence of Catakism is further evidenced by the fact that cats have become the number one domestic creature on Earth, despite the fact that not one single feline in all of recorded history has ever been observed doing one thing of practical value for one single human being (unless you consider lying in the sun and licking their own fur to be of benefit to humans). Whereas dogs *doggedly* insist on protecting us, providing us exercise, tracking down our criminals, rescuing us from fires and avalanches, sniffing out diseases and illegal drugs, guarding our homes and businesses, and going to battle with us, cats insist on sleeping, slow-blinking, and staring at things that don't exist.

It is the very fact that Cat steadfastly refuses to serve Man in any way, shape, or form that demonstrates how one-sided humanity's relationship with cats really is. Humans do the revering. Cats are content to be the object of that reverence. Catakism is the perfect marriage of a creature with an endless need to kneel at the feet of something greater than itself (Man; see above) and a creature with an endless need to be knelt before (Cat; see the rest of this book).

At some point in our coevolution, Cat, seeing Man's innate drive to grovel, graciously agreed to be Man's eternal adulation recipient. In return, she asked only that Man feed Her, attend to Her toiletry needs, speak to Her in an unreasonably high-pitched voice eighteen hours a day, continuously parade new toys in front of her, and cater to each and every one of Her lifestyle preferences.

Thus was Catakism born.

Signs of a Catakist

If you're a Catakist, some or all of the following apply to you:

- ❧ You would rather saw off your own legs and commando crawl to the bathroom than remove a sleeping cat from your lap.
- ❧ Every trip to Costco, your first purchase is four cases of Fancy Feast Mornings Soufflé with White Meat Chicken, Garden Veggies and Egg. If you have any cash left over, you grab a five-gallon drum of Kirkland corned beef hash for the humans.
- ❧ Your goodnight rituals with Bootsy routinely outlast your husband's Viagra.
- ❧ You devote 5 hours of every day to sleep, 6 hours to work, and 13 hours to the posting and emailing of cat videos, cat memes, cat photos, cat GIFs, cat emoticons, cat apps, and cat snippets of wisdom.

- After watching *Extreme Cat Hoarders* on TV, you turn to your mate and ask, "When are they going to show the crazy stuff?"
- Only 25 percent of the surface area of your home is *not* occupied by cat trees, cat beds, litter boxes, cat scratching posts, cat hidey-holes, cat walkways, cat hammocks, cat feeders, cat toys, and cat swings; 100 percent of the surface area of your home *is* covered in cat fur.
- You've left your college kid stranded at the bus station on Christmas Eve in a snowstorm because you were caught up arranging your kitty's presents under the Christmas tree.
- You always upgrade to the latest iPhone as soon as it's released so you can take *better* videos of your cat sleeping (and email them *faster* to everyone on your contacts list).
- You're put off when your date/mate uses his fingers to grab a french fry from your plate at a restaurant, but you think nothing of letting Simba bury his face in your ice cream dish.
- When you enter a home that doesn't stink of litter box, you turn to your companion and whisper, "Does this place smell funny to you?"

And on and on it goes.

Think of it this way. If an alien anthropologist were to visit your home and objectively *cat*-alog its contents and your behaviors, would she not unhesitatingly conclude that kitties were your central object of religious devotion? And if you thought about it for a minute, would you not be forced to agree?

Humanity's over-the-top obsession with cats—in our homes, in the media, on our computers and smartphones, in our bookstores and boutiques—has escalated into a full-blown belief system that belongs in the same *cat*-egory as the great philosophies and religions of the world.

That belief system is Catakism.

Okay then, let's not pussyfoot around this. What, exactly, *is* Catakism?

II. Catakism Categorized
In its fullest definition, Catakism is:

> *The deep and reverent belief in Cat as master, guru, mentor, sage, and ridiculous ball of cuteness.*

A Catakist walks a strange line. On one hand, she recognizes the infinite superiority of Cat to Man. This is evidenced by behaviors such as:

1. **Constantly seeking the "blessing" of cats.** When a Catakist enters a home where a cat resides, her first act, before speaking to the humans, is to seek out the resident feline and pay homage. If the cat snubs her and/or runs away, the human feels deeply flawed and shamed. If the feline allows the human to rub under her neck or behind her ears, the human feels validated and affirmed. If the feline—blessing of all blessings—approaches the *human*, purrs, and rubs against her, the human feels like a chosen disciple and is ready to purchase a saffron robe and a begging cup and commence a lifetime of monastic devotion.

2. **Constantly trying to please cats.** A Catakist dedicates all of her free time and disposable income to eliciting signs of approval from her cat. She is on a never-ending quest to find the perfect cat food, cat snack, cat toy, cat furniture, and cat experience that will engage her feline's attention for more than half a second. Ninety percent of the time, of course, the cat rejects the offering of the human— making a point, for example, of playing with the bag the toy came in rather than the toy itself. But when a cat actually eats the food, plays with the toy, or watches the DVD the human has purchased,

the human enters a state of euphoria so extreme she begins speaking in tongues (e.g., "Puddy-wuddums *loves* her diddly-boojums!")

3. **Deferring to cats' tastes and preferences.** The average Catakist's home is a temple to Cat, with all lifestyle choices being made so as to protect the comfort zone of the resident feline. Everything from the volume of the TV, to the brightness of the lighting, to the placement of the furniture, to the thread count of the bed sheets is orchestrated to ensure maximum kitty comfort. (Shoes, of course, are forbidden in the devotee's home lest the human create a single decibel of sound that might disturb one of the cat's sixteen daily naps and cause it to do the tail-in-the-air, stiff-legged trot to another room.)

4. **Behaving obsequiously toward cats.** The behavior of the average cat disciple around felines is similar to that of a psychotic third-world dictator's butler. There is a servile, fawning, overly-eager-to-please, I-beg-you-not-to-kill-me quality to all of the human's behaviors—from the high-pitched, placating baby talk voice she uses to the delicate way she maneuvers in and out of the cat's personal space—that clearly establishes the power hierarchy between the two species.

On the other hand, a polar opposite reality seems to be at play. Catakists consider cats insanely cute and funny, too. All it takes to render a Catakist useless for hours is to:

- email photos of cats sitting in boxes, teacups, or any container that's too small for their bodies
- start a "My cat is so weird, he . . ." conversation
- place a book of cat cartoons or cat jokes within arm's reach
- say the word "kitten"
- write the word "kitten"
- mime the word "kitten"
- acknowledge in any way, shape, or form the fact that kittens exist.
- suggest the possibility that there might be a cute kitten (i.e., *a kitten*) within a 40-mile radius
- display a YouTube video of cats jumping in surprise, cats getting too close to camera lenses, cats bouncing crazily off walls, cats sneaking up on inanimate objects, cats knocking things off shelves, cats miscalculating leaps, cats whacking other animals on the nose, cats getting involved with toilets, cats hiding in bags, cats sliding on polished floors, cats watching popcorn pop, cats interacting with computer printers, and/or cats doing pretty much any activity imaginable, including sitting, sleeping, staring, or frowning

So, while Catakists hold felines in the esteem of full-blown deities, they also spend hours of every day wetting themselves with laughter as they browse through social media pages looking for photos of cats wearing helmets carved from pieces of fruit.

How does anyone straddle this strange line between adoration and absurdity, between reverence and ridicule, between sacredness and sappiness? Hard to say, but all Catakists do it.

In fact, we might even say that it's in this weird space between opposites that Catakism thrives.

III. The Cat-a-gorical Imperative

Every belief system needs a core principle that its believers can embrace. For Catakists, it is the *Cat-a-gorical Imperative.*

Perhaps this term sounds vaguely familiar. If you studied philosophy in college, then one of two things is probably true: (1) you were a philosophy major, in which case you are now enjoying a stimulating career at Hooters, or (2) you needed to fill an elective, in which case your experience with Intro to Philosophy had about as much lasting effect on you as an expired suppository. Either way, you've undoubtedly forgotten the Categorical Imperative.

The Categorical Imperative basically said do unto others as you would have them to do unto you. It provided everyone, regardless of belief, with a universal way of making moral decisions. In a similar way, the Cat-a-gorical Imperative provides Catakists with a universal way of treating cats.

The Cat-a-gorical Imperative:

Treat every cat you meet as if it were simultaneously the King of the Jungle, the Dalai Lama, and Hello Kitty.

In other words, respect a cat's infinite nobility, pay it deep spiritual homage, and be endlessly amused by everything it does.

This is the strange contradictory place where Catakists comfortably dwell, 24/7.

IV. At the Mercy of Meow–Catakism: The Belief System

To appreciate the true depth and power of Catakism, it helps to look at how humans practice other important beliefs in their lives. Humans *say* they believe in many moral and spiritual principles, such as Love Thy Neighbor, Keep the Sabbath Holy, Thou Shalt Not Covet Thy Neighbor's Goods, and, of course, good ol' Do Unto Others . . . but they tend to be *just* a bit selective when it comes to putting those beliefs into practice—and they are willing to abandon those beliefs at the slightest sign of a challenge. For example:

- 😺 I *tried* the whole Love Thy Neighbor thing, but then Carl next door sprayed lawn clippings on my driveway.
- 😺 I *tried* to keep the Lord's Day holy, but then my team got scheduled to play the ****ing Patriots on Sunday Night Football!
- 😺 I *tried* Do Unto Others as You Would Have Them Do Unto You, but I found that for me, personally, I prefer Screw You, But Give Special Treatment to Me. That's just me, though.
- 😺 I *tried* Do Not Covet Thy Neighbor's wife, but *damn*!

Not so with Catakism.

Though Catakists don't consider their way of life a "belief system" as such, they are actually more consistent with their reverence and devotion to Cat than they are with their most devoutly professed beliefs.

For example, you never hear a Catakist shout, "Hey cat—yeah, *you*—move your fat, furry a**!"

You never hear a Catakist grumbling, "Why does my cat have all the nice stuff while I'm slaving away to make ends meet?"

You never see a Catakist fail to observe National Cat Day, her feline's birthday, the anniversary of the day she brought said feline home, or the anniversary of the theatrical release of *Cats*—with all of the attendant rituals and solemnity.

And you never, NEVER see a Catakist go twenty-four hours without uploading, downloading, sharing, or posting at least a dozen *hilarious* and/or *adorable* cat memes.

Day in and day out, all around the world, people organize their lives around Catakism with a fervor and consistency a medieval monk would envy. Catakism may not be a religion in the strictest sense of the word, but one would never know it by watching the behavior of believers! Jobs may come and go, relationships may begin and end, but belief in Cat is one thing that never wavers in a Catakist's life.

No *bad* behavior that a cat ever exhibits, such as leaving you a dissected mouse on the welcome mat, turning your potted plants into indoor outhouses, burying its claws in your flesh, vomiting on the dinner table during Seder, or demonstrating the theory of gravity by tipping your wineglass onto the white carpet, is enough to shake a Catakist's faith.

The point is this: We claim to practice many noble and worthy beliefs, but we do not practice those beliefs consistently, day in, day out. On the other hand, Catakists practice their kitty beliefs and rituals with unwavering devotion.

V. Cuddled into Servitude–A Brief History of Cats and Humans

In order to understand how Catakism evolved on Earth, one must explore the origins of Man's relationship with Cat.

It is believed that cats first began gravitating to human settlements when these two-leggeds first started collecting grains, nuts, and berries. Man's food storage bins attracted small mammals, such as rats and mice, in great numbers, making them easy to catch. Cats quickly realized it was much more pleasant to sit in the sun and snag mice like doughnuts from a Krispy Kreme conveyor belt than to chase wild prey through the jungle where things like failure, discomfort, and inconvenience could sometimes occur.

Man, for his part, came to realize that you could not enjoy nuts and grains if they no longer exist. And so began what *should* have been a long and mutually beneficial relationship between cats and humans (with only the mice saying, "Remind me again, what are *we* getting out of this?").

But somewhere around the middle of day three, Cat came back to Man with a counterproposal, "You know, I'm starting to realize that staking out your grain silo all day takes a lot of concentration and energy.

And I'm not all that crazy about the taste of live rodent, if I'm being honest. It's kinda gamey, actually. I'm wondering if you could cook it in a flavorsome broth for me while I curl up in the corner over there and nap."

To which Man replied with an enthusiastic, "Absolutely! Do you want me to cut it up into bite-size morsels too?"

Thus began the one-way, servant-and-master relationship that is the root of modern Catakism.

VI. Catakism in History

Though Catakism has only now been identified and named as a major worldwide faith, it has been practiced for millennia in diverse cultures around the world. People have long attributed magical powers and beliefs to cats, such as: a cat sneezing is a good omen; a white cat is a sign of good luck; when entering a building, one must always let a cat enter first; and, the lesser known and more recent, to fail to open a shared cat video on one's smartphone brings seven years of bad luck.

Here are a few examples of Catakism in history and religion:

Cyprus

For many years, historians believed the Ancient Egyptians first domesticated cats 4,000 years ago (and began worshipping them 3,999 years and 364 days ago). We now know that cats and humans became cozy with one another much earlier than this. Recently, skeletons of a human and a cat, buried together more than 9,500 years ago, were discovered in Cyprus in an ancient dwelling.

What most of us may not be surprised to learn is that the human was wearing a toga embroidered with the message, "Proud Cat Daddy." On the wall was a primitive drawing of a kitten dangling from a tree branch, with the carved inscription, "Hang In There." Early Catakists.

Egypt

Egyptians may not have been the first to worship cats, but they were certainly the most enthusiastic. Ancient Egyptians believed that all cats were owned by the Pharaoh, making it punishable by death to harm or kill a cat. This belief was brought home in a true story reported by Herodotus. A Roman soldier in Egypt *accidentally* killed a cat, and a huge mob of angry Egyptians took to the streets to demand the soldier's head. Eventually, the Pharaoh himself had to step forward and say,

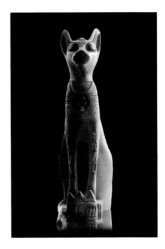

"Jeez, people, take it down a notch. It was a freakin' accident. And maybe back off on the lattes just a hair, too."

In ancient Egypt, when a cat died, all members of the household shaved off their eyebrows because . . . yeah.

Islam

The cat is revered in Islam both for its cleanliness and its relationship to the prophet Mohammed. Mohammed loved the kitties, yes he did. There is a famous story in which the prophet was summoned to a prayer meeting, but there was a cat sleeping on the sleeve of his robe. And so, rather than wake the cat, he cut off his sleeve.

This extreme story is known to Catakists as *normal* everyday behavior.

Christianity

Jesus Christ was also known to have a great affinity for cats. The controversial Gospel of the Holy Twelve records the following:

"And as Jesus entered into a certain village he saw a young cat which had none to care for her, and she was hungry and cried unto him, and he took her up, and put her inside his garment, and she lay in his bosom."

Less well known is the ending of the story:

"And then didst Jesus take the kitty home in his robe and, plucking the foil wrapper from his falafel, fashioned from it a crude cat toy. Yea, verily didst the Lord watch the kitty bat the ball of foil about until the tenth hour, at which time he didst offer the kitty sweet cream, a bed made of the finest goose down, and a light snack of kippered herring and sautéed chicken giblets."

Yes, the most enlightened beings among us have all been cat people. Felinity is next to Divinity!

VII. Meow You See Me, Meow You Don't—Evidence of Catakism Around Us

Brethren, let us pray.

Now that the cat is out of the bag about kitty worship being a worldwide, mainstream phenomenon, the time has come to openly celebrate our feelings and beliefs about Cat. The time has come to raise Catakism to a fur-mal belief system that stands nose, tail, and whiskers alongside all the other great faiths of the world.

And that is exactly what we see happening in the world today. Victor Hugo once said, "Nothing is as powerful as an idea whose time has come." (A random cat *owner* once said, "Nothing is as powerful as a litter box whose time to be cleaned has come.")

Here are some signs of the rising tide of Catakism in today's world:

- National Cat Day observances
- the cat food aisle in the supermarket taking up more room than the produce and bakery departments combined
- a constant stream of kitty-themed books on bestseller lists, with cats often paired with random items such as cheeseburgers, tiny hats, cupcakes, murder plots against you, and homeless guys named Bob

- more kitties than porn on the Internet
- no, really, more kitties than porn on the Internet!
- the fact that this >.< is enough to make you see a cat
- the actual existence of a product called Fancy Feast® *Medleys* White Meat Chicken Primavera Paté with Garden Veggies and Greens
- the fact that a grocery store employee will point you to the above product without bursting into tears of laughter
- entire stores and businesses with names like Meowington's, The Cat's Pajamas, Meowiott Hotel, Chez Mieux, Kitten Kaboodle, Sandy Claws, and Kitty City
- cat flakes—don't pretend you don't know what they are, you no-good work-shirker you
- the fact that more people can name a certain cat with a grumpy face than the vice president of the United States or the head of any foreign nation
- cat toys more elaborate and high-tech than the latest-model Tesla
- the recent replacement of the iron-shaped playing piece in Monopoly® with a cat
- new social phenomena, such as cat cafés in Japan (where you pay to go and be with cats), cat therapy, and cat feng shui

The way we humans feel about cats is undeniable. The jury is still out on how cats truly feel about us, though. All cat owners insist, "My cat loves me." But this claim is usually made with the same desperately hopeful look on the face as when saying, "My family loves my cooking," and "I'm pretty well set for retirement."

Humans adulate cats, revere them, idolize them, adore them, praise them, dress them in tutus, and photograph them. To say that humans love cats is like saying sharks have a scholarly interest in fresh meat. Humans *obsess* over cats. However, because their obsession is second nature to them, they are often unable to see the degree to which Catakism has taken over their lives.

This helps explain how an otherwise mentally healthy individual can slowly transform from a casual cat enthusiast to a crazy cat lady without realizing that any change has taken place.

VIII. Believers and DICKs

As with any religious or ideological belief system, there are varying degrees of belief and commitment to Catakism, but there is one fundamental distinction that must be understood right from the outset so that we may speak a common language. That is, there are believers and nonbelievers. Believers come in many degrees of Catakistic faith, from kitten smitten to crazy cat lady, while all nonbelievers are considered DICKs (Doesn't Idolize Cats and Kittens). It should also be noted that some people are actually allergic to cats. These people need our support, our pity, and our Benadryl, for they can never fully attain enlightenment or salvation.

DICKs range from those who just don't get the cat thing to those who loathe and detest cats. Some DICKs support their friends' and spouses' Catakistic faith but prefer not to practice themselves. Others actively avoid cats.

The state of DICKhood is a self-reinforcing one. DICKs distance themselves from cats. That's because all cats instantly recognize a DICK when one walks into the room. When a cat senses a

DICK, she becomes aloof, rigid, frightened, avoidant, or downright hostile. This confirms the DICK's belief that "cats are unaffectionate, standoffish, disloyal, and only in it for themselves." Which, in turn, causes the DICK to behave like a dick the next time he or she sees a cat. Which, in turn, causes the cat to . . . well, you get it.

However, when a Catakist enters a room, even the grumpiest of grumpy cats becomes a melted ball of wriggles, stretches, and purrs.

The only way the eternal cycle of DICKhood can be broken is when a cat chooses a two-legged to move into his/her home and cures the DICK of their DICKliness by sheer force of will. That former DICK is now ready to convert to Catakism by means of a formal Cat Mitzvah.

IX. The Catma of Catakism—The Ninefold Path

All religions have guidelines for believers. Catakism, too, has its collection of catma (can't call it dogma now, can we?), or moral and spiritual guidelines. One of the central pieces of catma is the Ninefold Path of Catakism.

Nine is a sacred number in Catakism. It represents the number of lives a cat is said to have, the number of cats owned by the average crazy cat lady, and the number of times the average crazy cat lady has had to move for having too many cats.

How the Ninefold Path came to be shared with Man is a subject of some debate. There are many myths, but here are two of the most popular *tails*:

Myth #1: A fat cat was observed to be sitting motionless under a bodhi tree for forty days and forty nights. The citizens of the nearby village mistakenly assumed the cat had attained enlightenment when, in fact, it was just watching a bird's nest. The cat imparted the Ninefold Path to the eager village people so they would go away and not bother it anymore.

Myth #2: A kitty Zen master came before his human disciples and sat, wearing a serious expression on his face and a slice of bread around his head. The disciples were not sure whether the bread was intended to be funny or not, and the Zen master gave no clue as to his intent or desire. He simply sat there, staring impassively. At last, one of the disciples could stand it no more and burst out with a loud guffaw. At this point, the Zen master gave the student a stern look and handed him a scroll containing the Ninefold Path. "Read this and come back when you are truly ready to learn," he said. And then the master departed, never to be seen again.

It is said that believers who follow the entire Ninefold Path can eventually become Ascended Masters of Catakism . . . or at least Keepers of Contented Kitties.

Ninefold Path Guidepost #1

*To ridicule, laugh at, or make light
of a cat is to forfeit thy eternal soul.*

Although it is perfectly permissible to giggle warmly at posters of kittens with confetti stuck to their fur, chortle heartily at photographs of cats wearing bunny ears, and laugh insanely at videos of determined cats attempting to place themselves in containers much too small for their bodies, it is never, ever, ever acceptable to laugh at a live cat. Cats must be treated with absolute dignity, no matter how badly they judge their leaps to high pieces of furniture or how hilariously they get household objects stuck to their heads.

A cat is, first and foremost, King of the Jungle. A cat is secondarily a goddess worthy of devotion. Only a distant third is a cat a source of entertainment for humans. Woe betide the mortal who gets that order wrong.

THE BOOK OF KNEAD

Cats knead us. We need cats.

I. Knead

It all begins with knead. Cats *knead* us. And we convince ourselves that cats *need* us. But it is really we who need them. Catakism's power stems from our deep and abiding need for kitties in our lives.

Let us look at the act of kneading itself—that mysterious cat behavior in which a cat's claws puncture our flesh, like a meat tenderizer into a steak, while purring loudly—for this act encapsulates the heart of the human–feline relationship and sets the stage for Catakism.

Kneading is a process that universally unfolds in several steps:

1. **The cat locates the softest part of the human's body.** This could be the thigh, the belly, the breast; as a general rule, finding a soft spot on a human is not particularly challenging. It's important to understand, though, that as the cat seeks a literal soft spot on the human, it is symbolically seeking an *emotional* soft spot, the place where the human is least guarded and defended. For that is where it gains its point of entry into the human's psyche.

2. **The cat begins applying pressure** on the human's body like a Swedish masseur named Sven. Just as a human kneads dough

to turn it into bread, the kitty kneads the *human* to turn *her* into dough. The rhythmic up-and-down action of alternating paws does an end-run around the rational mind and lulls the human into a state of delirium.

3. **The cat emits the loudest purr in its repertoire,** further hypnotizing the human and rendering her incapable of defending herself physically or mentally. To seal the deal, the cat turns on the "soft eyes" and the slow blinks, which reduces the human's vocabulary to two words: "Yes, meow-ster?"

4. **The cat releases its weapons.** Once the human is sufficiently lulled into mental surrender (average time required: 5 seconds), the cat unleashes its hidden weapon. It flips open the tiny switchblades hidden in its paws and commences to repeatedly lacerate

the human it professes to love, over and over, with needle-sharp mini spears.

Does the human scream and fling the cat across the room? No. The human submits, and the cat literally *has its hooks* into her. The human now *wants* to be kneaded—and needs to be needed—by the cat.

And so begins that exquisite marriage of love and pain called "cat ownership."* Think *Fifty Shades of Gray Tabby*.

* As noted earlier, no human owns a cat.

II. Need

Although humans need cats, we also possess a strange entity known as an ego. This delicate and fragile entity feels threatened at all times, so it protects and defends itself by making the human feel vastly more important than he/she actually is. In Catakism, this manifests with the human convinced that the cat needs *her*, rather than the other way around.

However, cats are totally fine without humans. They can feed themselves, bathe themselves, house themselves, have kittens without midwives, and, yes, even poop all by themselves, all without any human intervention. This thought is horrifying to the human. After all, if the kitty doesn't *need* the human, the kitty might decide to leave, and that would be cat-astrophic!

And so the dedicated Catakist convinces herself that kitty has a huge list of highly specialized needs that only the human can fulfill.

Cats need protection and shelter. The first thing a Catakist tells herself is that a cat needs the shelter and protection of a human home to survive. Because out there in the savage wilds of suburban Sunnyvale, the cat might be attacked and eaten by any number of predators, such as . . . thinking, thinking . . . dum de dum. Pterodactyls?

Okay, yes, in some places there are wild animals, such as coyotes, that occasionally prey on cats, but cats are pretty much the apex predator in most environments where humans also live. Just ask the local blue jays, mice, and even dogs.

Yet humans are so convinced that kitties need protective custody that they basically place them under house arrest 24/7. Many Catakists turn their homes into Cattica, Whisker's Island, Alcatraz, Pawshank . . . only permitting their cats to explore a tiny outdoor exercise yard using any means possible short of barbed wire to keep them contained. But up until about seventy years ago, many house cats roamed freely outdoors and they were just fine.

The *real* reason many Catakists are so protective is not that Cat can't fend for herself, but that, given an option, Cat might take her chances living with the "other" crazy cat lady down the street. And every once in a while a cat does just that—packs its bags, collects its security deposit, and moves in with the Franklins around the corner—just to remind the humans that Cat has a mind of her own and decides where to live.

Cats need gourmet food. Catakists actually believe that Cat is incapable of eating without human intervention. Not only is Cat unable to feed herself, thinks the Catakist, but she is also a highly finicky, specialized eater that requires a nonstop variety of cooked and prepared gourmet dishes such as Flaked Tilapia in Consommé, Turkey Soufflé, Duck and Wild Rice in Gravy, Extreme Tuna Surprise, and Grilled Chicken and Prawns with Spring Vegetables. Dog food comes in the form of "chow" and "kibble," but cat food comes in the form of paté, mini-fillets, flakes, shreds, premium cuts, and entrées. Catakists, in fact, won't feed their cat any food that doesn't have an accent mark over one of the words.

The most casual glance at a nature show, however, reveals that cats are the most exquisitely designed hunters in the animal kingdom. Turns out, if you don't offer them a jeweled chalice filled with Yellowfin Tuna Florentine, they will happily rip a chipmunk into "gourmet shreds" and eat it—horror of horrors—without the giblet gravy. No, says the Catakist, not my Snowball!

Cats need pampering. Despite the fact that cats take better care of themselves than the average hotel chain heiress—some spending up to 50 percent of their waking time cleaning and grooming themselves (fact)—Catakists tell themselves that their  cats require 24-hour *human* pampering. This may be in the form of thrice-daily brushings; special blankets, beds, and indoor play areas; hypoallergenic bathing wipes; professional groomings; "nail *pawlish*"; servings of warm milk in crystal stemware; special platforms from which to watch the birds outside; and bejeweled accessories.

Nine Signs That You Might Be Spoiling Your Cat

1. Passersby ring your doorbell asking if they can rent the cat house in your backyard as a summer home.
2. Your cat gets an iPad upgrade before you do so it can play Cat Fishing 2 in super hi-res.
3. Your cat's litter box not only cleans itself, but also offers the user a steamed towel and an assortment of eau de toilette.
4. Your cat has begun to resemble a hassock with feet.
5. Your cat has its own online account at Socks Fifth Avenue.
6. Your cat occasionally tips you for your services.
7. All of your furniture has built-in tunnels.
8. You worry about how your cat is going to rate your service skills on your annual staff evaluation.
9. "Repair the cat elevator" is higher on your to-do list than "Feed the kids."

Cats Need to Be Carried. Thirty million years of evolution have crafted the cat into the most finely tuned athlete in the entire animal kingdom. And yet some Catakists believe that cats are incapable of even rudimentary self-locomotion. In fact, 37 percent of Catakists believe they must *carry* Twinkles from the couch to the bird-watching window to the feeding platform to the feather bed.

Not only must a cat be carried from point A to every point B—and placed in a stroller when going outdoors—it must also be picked up and set down with the delicacy reserved for handling live grenades.

Cats Need to Be Entertained. Cats are Zen masters who require no external stimulation whatsoever, but Catakists provide an endless parade of cat toys, cat shows, and cat devices before Mr. Tibbs all day long, despite Mr. Tibbs's cat-aclysmic lack of interest.

Cats don't sleep 17.5 hours a day because they're tired—we make sure they don't have to do anything to tucker themselves out—it's because they want to avoid our endless barrage of mechanical fish and electronic mouse-noise generators.

Cats Need Poop Intervention. Perhaps the greatest way humans have inserted themselves into the natural processes of cats is the invention of the litter box. Evidently, humans believe that cats are not capable of pooping on their own, and so they have created a multi-billion-dollar industry based on the collecting and disposing of cat doo-doo.

We have convinced ourselves that without spring-breeze-scented, miracle-clumping, scoopable, multi-cat litter box crystals with odor-eliminating carbon, poor Cat would be forced to hold it in throughout eternity. We are genuinely shocked to learn that when not provided with luxury toilet facilities and bathroom attendants, a cat will poop on something we like to call the ground.

And so, yet another paradox of Catakism is revealed. On one hand, we worship our felines as superior beings, but on the other hand we

tell ourselves that cats can't eat, sleep, walk, or poop without our help, which places them somewhere below the garden slug on the evolutionary scale.

Of course, all our posturing about cats needing *us* is just a smokescreen for the fact that we desperately need our kitties.

III. Kitty Misses Me

One way humans deal with their attachment to Cat is by telling themselves that their kitty suffers from separation anxiety when the two are not together. Humans feel extremely guilty about leaving their kitties home alone for a few days or even a few hours.

In order to help ease kitty's fictional separation anxiety, humans do things like leave *Too Cute: Kitties* on TV "for kitty" when they go out for the evening, leave an electronic fish game running, or leave an article of clothing with the human's scent on it for the kitty to sleep on. When they're going to be away for more than a day, some Catakists actually call and talk to their kitty via the answering machine or send them mouse emojis on their kitty tablet devices.

But who really misses whom? Do cats really give a litter-lump about humans leaving them for a day or a week? No, as long as they have plenty of food and water, cats view their time away from the human as (warning, the following content may be disturbing) . . . a vacation!

Yes, without the human around, Cat can:

- walk through a room without being scooped up and asked, "Who's the sweetest kitty in the world? Bootsy is! Oh yes he is, oh yes he IS!"
- eat a meal at her leisure without a human face six inches away, anxiously asking, "Does Princess like her Trout Supreme? Mommy bought it special for her little one."
- enjoy a full twenty-four hours without being photographed in a hat of any kind
- experience *actual* silence, as opposed to *human* silence, which includes background music; televisions; beeping and pinging from electronic devices; footsteps; belches, sighs, groans, and stomach growls; clanging dishes and silverware; flushing toilets; blenders, choppers, and garbage disposals; electric fans; and, of course, spontaneous and unconscious outbursts of "Who's my snuggly wuggums?"

Because humans possess the aforementioned ego, though, they have a need to view separation anxiety as coming from the kitty. The truth is, when they leave their cat, it's *their own* anxiety that humans are sensing. The cat has no need to set his human's face as his smartphone's wallpaper so he can look at her all day when she is at work. The cat has no need to get a coffee mug custom-made with his human's face on it and the caption, "I love my Latina Longhair." In the human's absence, the cat has no need to post videos on YouTube of the human sleeping and wait anxiously for the "Cutest. Human. Ever." comments to start rolling in.

No, when the human is away, the cat will play.

IV. Every Pounce of Our Love: We Can't Be Without Them

For Catakists, cats provide a reason for living as well as the default focus for all of the love and attention in the household, and the Catakist simply doesn't know how to handle Cat's absence. Catakist couples, for example, get nervous when they don't have the cat around to serve as their relationship go-between. For without Whiskers around to talk to in a ridiculously high-pitched voice, they actually have to talk to *each other*.

V. Controlled by the Cuteness: Feline Attachment

Humans are attached to Cat like no other creature on Earth. American homes, for example, have more than ninety million cats, as opposed to

seventy to eighty million dogs. The greatest measure of human attachment, of course, is the way we spend our money. For example, spending patterns reveal that while humans may enjoy going to the movies, they are *attached* to their televisions; while humans may enjoy sushi, they are *attached* to pizza. Similarly, while humans enjoy cockatiels, ferrets, and lop-eared bunnies, they are *attached* to Cat.

According to Peteducation.com, the average cat owner spends between ten and twenty thousand dollars on a cat over its lifetime. This covers the initial purchase, spaying/neutering, food, litter, litter boxes, cat furniture, replacement of cat-damaged human furniture, window perches, cat beds, cat door construction, cat carriers, scratching posts, food dishes, grooming tools, fur-removing tape, carpet stain removers, flea control products, heartworm prevention, training (ha!) aids, routine vaccines, dental care, ear care, vitamins, and occasional boarding.

A Catakist views such mundane expenses as a mere starting point, adding further staple purchases such as:

- climate-controlled cat condos
- ergonomically designed cat grooming tools
- alternative therapies, such as aromatherapy; Shiatsu, Thai, traditional, and Tellington TTouch massages; Reiki; acupuncture; acupressure; and kitty chiropractics
- a 24-hour film crew for capturing cunning videos

And let's not forget all the cat toys, cat treats, cat costumes, and other purr-aphernalia that fills a Catakist's home from top to bottom.

VI. Feline Attachment Disorders
Feline attachment creates a number of mental, physical, emotional, and spiritual conditions that Catakists must guard against. Most

Catakists eventually contract one or more of these grave disorders and must seek treatment by a physician, cleric, or pet store owner.

Feline Deprivation Disorder (a.k.a. cat separation anxiety) affects most Catakists who are forced to endure more than forty-eight hours without playing with a cat, watching a cat video, or sharing photos of cats dressed in their finest. Symptoms include nausea, dizziness, a glazed look in the eye, and the proclivity to roll around on the floor batting a ball of yarn. When this syndrome appears in children, it's know as Juvenile Feline Deprivation Disorder (JFDD), for which there is only one cure: kittens, kittens, and more kittens.

Urine Nasal-blindness. Cat urine bears one of the strongest, most distinct, and least pleasant odors known to humanity. Catakists, however, are blissfully unaware of it. The human brain adapts to *any* stimulus it is constantly surrounded by, and when your home contains three litter boxes, a spraying tomcat, one Shadow Cat angry at its human for taking too long at the grocery store, an open-door policy on strays, *and* wall-to-wall carpets, then cat pee is like oxygen to you. You need an intervention—namely, someone with a working nose who will slap you back to your senses.

YouTubular Compulsivity. At first it was just a social thing. You enjoyed an occasional YouTube cat video with friends. But now it has turned into a dark compulsion that's threatening to ruin your life. You watch on your computer, your smartphone, your tablet, and your watch. You secretly store cat video files on your hard drive in case the Internet ever goes down, and you have backup devices in your desk drawer, under your bed, and even under the bathroom sink. When everyone is asleep, you stay up watching cat videos and endlessly typing "adorable" into comment boxes. You need help. Or at least a faster Internet connection so you can download more cat videos.

Feline Numerical Dysfunction. This disorder manifests as a mysterious inability to count cats. While sufferers retain their full mathematical competency in all other areas of life, they lose their ability to keep numerical tabs on how many kitties they own. Thus, as the Catakist acquires more and more felines, she tells herself, in her mind, that she has "at most two."

Researchers believe it is the fear of being classified as a crazy cat lady that often causes this common form of psychological denial. In other cases it may be an ultimatum from a spouse, such as, "If you bring home one more cat, I'm going to bulldoze the house, bury the rubble under six tons of pine tree air fresheners, and join a monastery."

Catatonic Navigational Disorder. Many Catakists develop a pathological inability to steer their automobiles away from pet stores, cat rescue centers, or cat cafés. Though they have every intention of just driving to the grocery store, they slip into an unconscious fugue state and then

find themselves sitting outside a feline-centric location with no memory of how they got there. Then, of course, they tell themselves, "Well, now that I'm here, I might as well go inside and take a quick peek."

VII. Man Makes Cat in His Image and Likeness: The Humanization of Cats

The ultimate sign of the powerful attachment to cats is people's insistence upon humanizing them. Catakists are so identified with their cats that they find it impossible to believe their kitty does not share a full range of human tastes, emotions, abstract thoughts, and behaviors. That's because when a Catakist looks into a cat's eyes, she sees another person looking back. So when the cat, for instance, awakens from a nap and looks at the human with a raised eyebrow, the Catakist imagines the cat is thinking something like, "I still haven't forgiven you for laughing at me yesterday when I mistook that piece of cellophane for a predator, but you can start to work your way into my good graces by *warming* my canned food for me today instead of feeding it to me cold from the fridge like I'm some kind of savage," when the kitty is really thinking, "What the hell are *you* looking at?"

Here are some of the most common ways diehard Catakists humanize kitties:

Dressing cats in human clothes. Cat lovers are endlessly fascinated by the sight of kitties dressed as humans, in spite of the fact that this custom brings only annoyance to felines. Seeing a kitty dressed in a pirate costume, granny dress, top hat, cowboy hat and bandanna, hoodie, sombrero, tam, witch hat, ballerina outfit, hipster getup, or a wig of any kind is enough to send Catakists into paroxysms of laughter. Cats wearing sunglasses are the all-time favorite. Perhaps this is because of the cool factor we attribute to cats, or maybe it's because sunglasses hide the look of raw disgust beaming from the cat's eyes as the human tries to wrangle said cat into an Elvis wig.

Cats doing random human activities. In addition to dressing cats in human clothes and projecting human thoughts onto them, Catakists are driven to spiritual ecstasy by looking at photos and videos of cats doing things like: "typing" on a computer keyboard, drinking at a bar, using a toilet, playing a piano, dancing on two legs, pushing a shopping cart, reclining in a La-Z-Boy," answering" a phone, opening doors, "talking," and reading.

Catakists also believe cats require full human treatment when it comes to boarding, grooming, feeding, entertaining, and celebrating their cats. Don't believe it? Read on . . .

Cat hotels. When a Catakist is forced—and force is usually required—to be away from his or her kitty, the only acceptable boarding choice is a full-scale cat hotel. Most of these facilities make the Waldorf look like a Red Roof Inn and feature things like four-poster beds, piped-in music, soft armchairs, plasma TVs, down pillows, private toilet facilities, climate control, and gourmet bedtime snacks.

Cat sitters. For the Catakist who can't bear to board their baby, there is an option of hiring a cat sitter who will come to the house and literally just sit there (because Catakists tell themselves that cats can't bear to be without human company for twelve whole hours). To Cat, this is known as "ruining my human-free vacation."

Special events. Catakists firmly believe that cats keep track of the human calendar and have a need to mark special events the same way humans do. This includes kitty birthday parties, complete with tuna birthday "cakes," and kitty Christmas card photo sessions, replete with (what else?) tiny Santa hats. But for the creative Catakist, this can also include celebrating holidays like Pink Floyd Day, which kitty celebrates by indulging in catnip; Bastille Day, when the cat is let out of the house for a day; and Cat Glory and Exaltation Day, which is pretty much every day of the year.

Catakists also celebrate the anniversary of their own Cat Mitzvah, the day they formally took on the mantle of Catakism.

Ninefold Path Guidepost #2

If you have money "left over" at the end of the month after paying your rent, utilities, and life insurance, you are not spending enough on your cat.

Some helpful ways to spend down: Consider, perhaps, adding a bidet to the litter box or a sound system to the kitty condo. Or maybe it's time for a new set of dining stemware in a shellfish theme. The one thing you don't want to happen is for your cat to see your checking account balance, inviting the question, "Why wasn't this money spent on me?" Good luck explaining that.

THE BOOK OF SURRENDER

Converting to Catakism

I. Cat-a-littic Conversion

To convert to Catakism is to dedicate one's life to serving Cat. The precise moment in time when one accepts that one's life is no longer one's own but now belongs to a purring, foot-high being covered in calico fur is known as a Cat-a-littic Conversion. It is the doorway through which lowly humans step in order to become practicing Catakists. A Cat-a-littic Conversion can be the culmination of a slow, gradual process or can occur in a single, blazing, spontaneous moment in time when one awakens with a purring kitten on one's chest and realizes the need to call in sick to work because moving that kitty is out of the question.

A Cat-a-littic Conversion is often surprising to the human who undergoes it. There may even be some resistance on the part of the convert. That's because many humans, particularly those with a penis, feel a certain amount of shame in admitting they have become rabid cat people. There is a popular belief that loving cats means you're not rugged. Worse, it means you may be a social misfit who values feline company over humans. Getting a cat is seen as a slippery slope to becoming a crazy cat lady. There is a prevalent idea that *cat people* are weird and eccentric.

All of these things are absolutely true, of course. But having a Cat-a-littic Conversion means saying, "Bring on the ridicule! I can't even hear it anymore. I love cats! In fact, I adore, idolize, and serve them."

Surrender Is Essential

For many, there is an ego struggle involved in accepting cats into their lives and their households. After all, humans like to believe *they* are the alpha hounds in every pack, so many two-leggeds begin their relationship with cats in a competitive posture. They get into a power struggle with the cat. They make vain pronouncements such as: "The cat is not in charge here," "This is our house, not the cat's," and "We need a new car more than the cat needs massage therapy."

Silly human.

Of course the cat is in charge.

Converting to Catakism means coming to a place of acceptance not only that one can't live without one's cat, but also that the cat is in charge and is going to dominate one's life from this point forward. Becoming a true Catakist means not only *accepting* this reality, but also *embracing* it.

Surrender is the word here.

II. Some Common Conversion Scenarios

Everyone surrenders to Catakism in his or her unique way, but there are some classic scenarios that occur repeatedly:

"Hey DICK, I live here now" (Cat spontaneously moves into human house). Many humans believe themselves to be dyed-in-the-wool DICKS—cat-*haters*, even—when they are, in fact, simply "cat naïve." They don't yet know the Power of the Pussycat. Until one day, when *that* cat shows up on their back porch and announces, in its own unique way, "I live here now. Deal with it." Sometimes this kitty "guest" is a total sweetie pie, who quickly wins the DICK over by sheer force of its cuteness. Other times it is a feral freakazoid who lurks in the shadows for months, slowly warming up to the human—and vice versa—as the human continues to feed it out of a sense of grim responsibility.

Either way, the cat is here to stay, and the human is doomed to fall in love. Some of the most dedicated Catakists in the world are convert-ed DICKs who were "adopted" by a cat who showed up at their home and ~~doggedly~~ cattedly changed their life.

"Can you watch my apartment when I'm away? Oh, by the way, I have a cat." Many humans become converts after being coerced into cat-sitting. They are asked to just feed the cat when a friend goes away. They take to this task with disdain, and the cat, at first, treats them the same way. Then one day, while en-joying an episode of *House of Cards* on the friend's Net-flix-enabled TV, the cat climbs onto the person's lap and gives it the soft eyes. When the homeowner returns, the cat must be pried from the new devotee's arms with a crowbar. The Cat-a-Littic Con-version has begun

"I've done my research, and a cat is the most logical pet choice." Some approach pet ownership with the cold logic of shopping for a washing machine. They do their due diligence, make their pros and cons lists, and conclude that a cat is the most appropriate pet for themselves and/or their children in keeping with their current lifestyle. They take on cat stewardship with unemotional detachment. Then, somewhere along the line, a subtle change starts to happen. They start hearing words like "smooshums" and "cuddly-boo" slipping out of their mouths, and before long they are buying tiny Santa hats and maniacally hitting the refresh button on their browser, waiting for the latest crop of kitten videos and memes to appear.

III. Levels of Belief

In any religious faith, believers come in varying degrees of intensity, from the casual Sunday churchgoer (who starts swearing at the other drivers in the church parking lot the moment the "love thy neighbor" sermon is over) to the raving fanatic who wears thumbtacks in his shoes as penance for the sin of being alive. Catakism is no different. Though all Catakists have a love of kitties that goes beyond what might be objectively considered sane and healthy, there is still a great range of commitment within the faith (as well as many believers who *ought* to be committed).

The hierarchy of belief in Catakism goes something like this:

DICK (Doesn't Idolize Cats and Kittens)—A DICK, of course, is not really a Catakist at all. But many DICKs, again, are simply cat-naïve people who have not yet gone through their Cat-a-littic Conversion. Many DICKs have a negative attitude toward kitties because of a misperception of cats as aloof or because of a bad experience they may have had with a cat as a child. Perhaps they were dragging a cat around by the tail and the kitty registered its objection by unleashing its claws. Perhaps their parents never exposed them to the Power of the Pussycat. Since there is no real legitimate reason to hate cats (ask any Catakist), all DICKs, by definition, have the potential to convert to Catakism.

Closet Catakist—There is often a period of time for DICKs in transition in which one slowly grows to love a cat but is reluctant to admit it to others. Suddenly one stops finding humor in "dead cat" jokes and starts finding oneself stroking a cat's cheeks when no one is looking. Thoughts like, "Cats are awful, but *this* one isn't so bad," begin to creep into his head. Then one day he finds himself sneaking downstairs at two in the morning to watch a *Too Cute! Kittens* marathon on Animal Planet, and he has to admit that he has a problem.

Kitten Smitten—Kittens are the gateway drug to cat addiction. Many humans are drawn into Catakism through an obsession with kittens. In fact, it is scientifically impossible for a human *not* to fall in love with kittens. The only way to preserve DICKhood is by ignoring kittens and pretending not to see them. Denial. For those who *do* pay attention to kittens—at pet stores, in videos, on TV shows—an obsession inevitably develops. Eventually, the human's defenses break down, and a kitten

is brought into the home. The kitten then grows into a cat, and the human grows into the cat's eternal servant.

Cat Person—At some point in the life of a developing Catakist, she puts her flag down firmly and publicly on the cat person side of the divide. This is a liberating coming-out-of-the-claws-et moment for many. Finally, this feline-crazed person can proudly don the "Hairy Pawter" T-shirt and start sending videos of her sleeping cat to everyone on her contacts list. Once one declares oneself a cat person, one has stepped onto the slippery slope to becoming a true cat addict, or *cattict*. It's only a matter of time.

Cattict—A cattict is a step beyond a mere cat person. The cattict has a bona fide addiction to kitties and cannot be away from them for more than a few hours without breaking into cold sweats. It is at the cattict stage where believers begin to make major lifestyle changes, such as quitting their jobs and canceling their gym memberships so they can spend more time at home with Mister Whiskers. This is also the stage at which many humans contract Feline Numerical Dysfunction and begin, deliberately or unconsciously, misreporting the number of cats they have. A cattict admits to loving cats but is in denial about the severity of his or her obsession. He or she may need to attend a Catticts Anonymous (CA) meeting.

The Nine Steps of Catticts Anonymous

1. *Admit that one is powerless over one's love of cats—and that one's life has become gloriously unmanageable because of this.*
2. *Come to believe that a power greater than oneself (i.e., Cat) is both responsible for one's addiction and also the key to one's sanity.*
3. *Make a decision to turn one's life over to Cat, as one understands Him (Persian, Siamese, American Shorthair, Devon Rex, et catera).*

4. *Make a searching and fearless inventory of the cupboards and cabinets in which one stores one's cat goodies. And then:*
5. *Admit to Cat the exact nature of one's shortcomings (not enough Friskies Buffet, not enough cat toys, not enough Feline Greenies™ Smartbites hair ball control tuna-flavored cat treats).*
6. *Humbly ask Cat to allow you to rectify said defects of inventory by breaking out the debit card, renting a small truck, and making a trip to Petco.*
7. *Make a list of all kitties one has laughed at, woken up from a nap, made loud noises in front of, or tried to move from one's lap and become willing to make amends to them all.*
8. *Make direct amends to such kitties whenever possible by letting them drink the tuna water out of the can, holding them up to the ceiling so they can catch the moth, and/or warming up the seat cushion so they can take it over the second you get up.*
9. *Seek, through constant chatting with one's cat(s) in the Feline Falsetto Frequency, to improve one's conscious contact with Cat as one understands Her (Maine Coon, Russian Blue, Japanese Bobtail, et catera).*

Alas, Cattics Anonymous has not gained much traction—not because there aren't millions of cattics (there are), but because no one shows up at the meetings. Cattics would rather stay home with their kitties.

Avowed Catakist—Though many cat devotees practice Catakism without even knowing it, there is a point at which one becomes an *avowed* Catakist and takes his or her spiritual practice to a whole new level. Once a human admits that they not only love cats, but are wildly obsessed with them, the dam of sanity collapses. This human now has no qualms about wearing her cat pajamas out in public, painting the front of her house to resemble a giant cat face, or making *What's New Pussycat* her phone's ringtone. And frankly, some qualms would be nice.

Crazy Cat Lady—Sooner or later, if a Catakist practices the faith long enough and seriously enough, she (or he) will become a crazy cat lady. Fear of becoming a crazy cat lady is actually the chief inhibiting force in Catakism. Without this healthy fear, most Catakists would become cat crazy decades sooner than they do. By the time devotees actually reach the crazy cat lady stage, they no longer care what friends, family, or boards of health think about them; their attitude is simply "bring on the cats."

Please note, becoming a crazy cat lady is not restricted by gender.

Ninefold Path Guidepost #3

Whether you are male or female, if you have three or more cats, you are a crazy cat lady. Admit it.

If you have only two cats right now, it's not too late to get help; go to the next Catticts Anonymous meeting in your area.

When a human has three or more cats, concepts like "valuable furniture" go out the window. Crazy cat ladies exhibit truly certifiable behavior, such as hosting tea parties for cats, firing buckshot at animal officers, and rewriting their wills to leave everything to the cats. And that's just their *public* behavior. Imagine what goes on in private.

Wait, on second thought, don't.

Cat Show Person—Every faith has its true extremists, and Catakism is no exception. That is the cat show person. This individual manages to hang onto a thin veneer of sanity, but in truth her obsession with cats, cat culture, cat breeding, cat equipment, cat humor, cat lore, cat healthcare, and cat networking runs even deeper than the crazy cat lady. She lives with no less than nine cats, but justifies this with the self-appointed title of "cat breeder" and referring to all kitties as "show cats."

Cat show people are the true religious fanatics of Catakism. They spend every weekend packing up their Igloo coolers and driving to venues like the Fairfax Grange Hall in Bakersfield and the Bubba's Pork Rinds Expo Center—their minivans bursting with the yowling of cats and the joyous odor of litter boxes—so they can stand beside other cat show people and, well, be at cat shows.

What is the purpose of cat shows?

No one outside the cat show world really knows. But die-hard Catakists organize their entire lives around them.

IV. Cathedrals of Catakism–Cat Shows

No study of Catakism would be complete without a peek at what goes on at cat shows.

While it's true that the private homes of cat lovers are the everyday "temples of Catakism," believers sometimes feel a need to gather together in a designated public place to celebrate their faith. Thus, the cat show was invented.

Here are several events of religious significance that take place at cat shows:

The judgment of souls—Almost every faith includes an element of moral judgment, and Catakism has its version—except that in Catakism, humans are judged vicariously through their cats.

A major component of every cat show is the ribbon competition. Participants submit their show cats to be judged by a cat show judge. This individual is the high cleric of Catakism, wielding immense power. She pokes and prods at each kitty, stretching it out like saltwater taffy, rubbing its fur, testing its reflexes, and examining its mouth and other assorted orifices. Then she announces a Best of Breed and a Best in Show.

The human participants await the judge's pronouncement as if it represented the eternal fate of *their own souls*. Winning a blue ribbon is seen as a tribute to their cat care skills and their dedication to Cat. Failure to receive even a yellow ribbon brings on harsh self-judgment and calls for penance; for example, seven days and seven nights with no cat videos.

Proselytizing—The cat show is the venue by which the serious Catakist attempts to recruit new members to the faith. She does this by promoting her chosen cat breed and selling purebred kittens to novices . . . provided they make it through the interview process and pass the background check she requires of potential buyers.

Cat shows are also the venue at which hardcore believers attempt to convert casual believers into raving fanatics. They do this by sharing obscure knowledge of weird feline urinary disorders, raving about the new IPaw9 that's about to be released, gossiping about the "bad" breeders in the business, and serving as a model of achievement—if you try hard enough, perhaps someday you, too, can spend every other weekend eating Lunchables off a folding table in a trade show hall while getting peppered with litter from the neighboring exhibitor's cat!

Acquisition of religious artifacts—Believers also come to cat shows to acquire rare objects of purr-aphernalia not available through retailers. Every cat show has a vendors' corner where one can obtain hard-to-find items, such as litter box odor alarms, membership in the Cat Consommé of the Month Club, Hello Kitty lingerie for humans, and cable-ready cat condos. This is also where one can network with kitty service providers, such as cat masseurs, cat astrologers, cat dieticians, cat casting agents, and cat portrait painters. Every Catakist takes a vow of poverty, and every cat show aims to help believers maintain those vows.

V. The Cat Mitzvah

Eventually, when one's faith and practice become strong enough, one will want to formalize one's conversion to Catakism by means of a cat mitzvah.

The time leading up to one's cat mitzvah is marked by intensive study and community service. Study can include watching extra cat videos and reading extra cat blogs, or doing scholarly research projects, such as "From Felix to Stimpy: The Changing Psychosocial Role of Cats in Animated Cinema."

Community service might entail changing the litter boxes at the local cat shelter or serving a gourmet canned meal of Herbed Duck Confit and Sweet Potatoes with Organic Botanicals to the local homeless kitty population (they won't be homeless for long; they'll soon be living at *your* home).

The cat mitzvah ceremony begins with a reading from the Purr-ah (the whole body of cat literature) and the formal acceptance of the Ninefold Path, and concludes with a rollicking celebration that may include:

- the ceremonial burning of the book *101 Uses for a Dead Cat*
- the ritual tasting of the cat food—come on, you've always wanted to
- the formal donning of the cat slippers (and informal abandonment of a normal social life)

VI. Considerations in Converting to Catakism

Taking on Catakism as one's faith is not necessarily an easy thing. After all, to be a Catakist means to devote roughly 97 percent of your waking moments to cuddling your kitty, taking photos of your kitty, talking to your kitty in the Feline Falsetto Frequency, videoing your kitty, posting videos of your kitty online, making Christmas cards of your kitty (this process starts around July and continues through December), hand-feeding your kitty, putting Scottish tams on your kitty, shopping for your kitty, grooming your kitty, and creating purr-formance art for your kitty. Something's got to go. And that something is all vestiges of a day job and healthy human relationships.

Many practical issues must be taken into consideration when making such a sweeping change in one's life.

Declaring one's faith—After one's cat-a-littic conversion, it is only fair to one's fellow humans that one come out of the claws-et and openly declare one's faith. This is especially true if one is in a committed relationship with a fellow human or plans to be in the near future. "Oh, by the way, I worship cats" is not something you should spring on a partner only weeks before the wedding, any more than, "You *do* know I'm a polygamist, right?" Catakism requires massive lifestyle adjustments—e.g., converting one's home into a giant cat cave, adjusting one's lung capacity to be able to breathe air with excessively high amounts of ammonia, and learning to live in monastic silence so as not to wake any sleeping cats—that many normal adults, DICKs or otherwise, might not be willing to make.

Intermarriage—It is strongly recommended that believers marry within the Catakism faith. Just as it would be difficult for a porn star and an Amish minister to enjoy a committed romantic relationship, it is hard for a mentally healthy and balanced individual to live with a Catakist.

Some possible intermarriage scenarios that can occur:

Catakist marries DICK. It is possible, under certain conditions, for a Catakist to live with a DICK. Those conditions are:

1. The DICK is extremely tolerant of cats. Extremely.

2. The DICK is willing to defer to the Catakist in all lifestyle decisions.
3. The DICK never complains about litter footprints on the dinner plates, the stench of uneaten Friskies® Seafood Medley in the air, or the inability to have marital relations due to the fact that the cat is watching and judging.
4. An ironclad prenup agreeing to the above stipulations is signed.
5. The DICK never, ever, ever makes the mistake of asking, "Who do you love more, me or the cats?" For if he does, the entire façade of the marriage will come crumbling down, and he will find himself dining on Long John Silver's takeout while getting his mail at the local Motel 6.

Catakist marries cat-hater. A cat-hater doesn't even get a *second date* with a Catakist, never mind a marriage proposal, so the only way this scenario could possibly occur is through an arranged marriage or an online-matchmaking situation in which the would-be spouse lies on his/her profile or fails to notice the "must love cats" warning at the top. This union will be cancelled faster than a sitcom called *TJ and the Talking Toaster*.

Catakist marries Dogtologist. The union of a Catakist and a Dogtologist can be a complicated one, since each thinks his or her animal reigns supreme. Two CEOs (Canine Executive Officer/Cat Executive Officer) in a household does not work. Something's gotta give. Namely, the dog person and his/her dog must be willing to allow the cat to be the alpha of the household. This state naturally occurs in most cases anyway, as most dogs melt into quivering terror in the presence of a self-confident cat (i.e., *any* cat). A dog that docilely accepts second fiddle status (whether he really means it or not) can be tolerated by a Catakist. The dog can even become a cat person's ally if he allows himself to be featured in adorable cat-sleeping-with-dog videos.

Catakist marries extreme Catakist. It can be a shock when a garden-variety Catakist realizes he has married someone who takes this thing *way* more seriously than he does. For someone at the kitten smitten stage to find himself paired with a crazy cat lady or cat show person, for example, is a test of faith that may be too daunting for the fledgling devotee. Or it might be just the spur he needs to move his faith to a higher level. One thing is for sure: the crazy cat lady is not going to say, "No problem, I'll get less crazy." The onus is on the moderate believer to either become more *psy-catic* or take his jingle balls and leave.

Catakist marries Catakist of a different sect. There are numerous sects within Catakism, just as there are within Judaism or Christianity. It can be difficult for, say, a member of the "Cat Is a Noble Savage Who Must Be Free to Roam the Forest at Night and Hunt and Procreate as He Sees Fit" sect to have a successful partnership with a member of the "Tinkerbell Must Sleep on a 1,000-Thread Count Silk Pillowcase or She Develops a Skin Rash and Needs to See Her Dermatologist" sect. There is a high divorce rate among such unions, as well as the potential for prolonged custody battles.

Which brings up another topic . . .

VII. An Important Ecumenical Issue Within Catakism
Though Catakism unites believers under a common banner, there is one key issue within the faith that tends to divide believers into camps.

Indoor vs. Outdoor: The Great Debate. Few topics can stir controversy amongst the faithful more than the question, "Should cats be allowed outdoors or kept indoors?" Those who believe in *outdoor cats* are holdovers from the ancient times (i.e., 70 years ago), when cats slept in barns and hunted for moles and sparrows. The *indoor cat* contingent represents the more progressive trend within Catakism. These are the Catakists who ardently believe that if kitties are allowed to stray more than two feet from a human home, they will encounter dogs, trucks, germs, other felines in heat, raccoons, tempting tree branches, neighbors with better cat food, and assorted other challenges that will harm them or lure them away from home. So they convince themselves that it is absolutely necessary that cats remain indoors 24/7, where humans can serve and cater to them day and night. To these people, the idea that cats should be allowed to roam outdoors is pure hair-esy.

VIII. Join the Meowvment!

In the end, though, the things that unite Catakists are far more numerous than the things that divide us. Those things are called Simba, Smokey, Boots, Smudge, Princess, Max, Grizabella, Jinx, and Mister Mistoffelees. It is our idiotic delight in all things feline that overrides any differences in how we express that delight.

Why do we humans feel such a compulsion to put cats on pedestals and give them our devotion, our service, and our high-pitched voices?

Well . . .

Why do we like garlic in our spaghetti sauce?

Why do we make a sound called "laughter" when we think something is funny?

Why do we fake yawn whenever there's an awkward silence in a conversation?

There is no answer to these eternal questions.

And there is no answer to the question of *why* when it comes to our obsession with kitties. Kitty obsession is just a given of human nature. It is bigger than us, and it has been so ever since humans and kitties first decided to hang out together tens of thousands of years ago. Kitty love is encoded in our DNA. Rather than analyze it, dissect it, and question it, perhaps all we need to do is *surrender* to it.

Catakism is the celebration of that surrender.

People think cat lovers are crazy, yet their numbers are growing. Catakism is sweeping the globe. Is everyone getting crazier, or is sanity simply being redefined? Has it now become normal to have cat acupuncturists on retainer and electronic cat ID-checkers on our pet doors (yes, they do exist)?

Whatever your opinion, it's time to join the Catakism movement! Millions already have. It's not complicated. Just honor the Ninefold Path, accept the fact that the cat is your master/guru, and dedicate your entire life to providing comfort and luxury for her.

Give up your antiquated notions that humans rule the planet. Give up your tired idea that your home belongs to you. Embrace the fact that you now play a servant role to an infinitely superior being.

Go ahead, line up at the local Freshpet® fresh pet foods cooler case and celebrate the fact that from now on Puffball will eat better than your two-legged family members.

Go ahead, sign up for kitty Reiki courses at the local yoga center so that you can perform daily energy healings on Twinkles.

Go ahead, spend your entire tax refund on liposuction for Princess so she won't be saddled with negative body-image issues.

That's only the beginning of what you will be doing in service to the Divine Feline.

What you'll get in return is the company of a glorious, furry being who loves you, depends on you (though she won't admit it), watches Animal Planet with you, and warms your lap like a living, breathing heating pad every night—and, yes, judges you for the awkward way you laugh.

THE BOOK OF CATTITUDE

Dictators of the Fur

I. Cattitude Defined

Cats have been able to create a master–servant relationship with humans, where so many other animals have failed. How have cats managed to *persuade* humans to willingly and gratefully do all of the care and feeding, all of the adoring, all of the spending, all of the litter box maintenance, and all of the work?

Cattitude.

Cats exude an attitude that commands servitude and adulation. Cattitude encapsulates all of the traits we worship in royalty, movie stars, rock stars, and professional athletes all rolled into one. And since we humans have proven ourselves powerless under the spell of celebrity even when it is on a TV set, a magazine page, or an iPad, what chance do we stand against a real live *celebrity* boldly licking its crotch in the middle of our living room?

When a cat walks into a room, a red carpet spontaneously unrolls at its feet, a spotlight follows it across the floor, and paparazzi appear to snap photos while a saxophone solo plays in the background. Okay, maybe not in reality, but in the mind of the Catakist, it's purr-fectly paws-ible.

Cats are so confident in their worship-worthiness, they literally put themselves on a pedestal. They will automatically sit on the highest horizontal surface in the room, even if it's just a paperback book lying on a table, so that the lesser species in the room can more easily pay homage.

Just try *not* to worship a cat. Dare you. It isn't easy.

Cattitude is why.

Cattitude is an exquisite blend of:

Superiority—A cat never exhibits the slightest doubt as to where it stands in relation to every other living thing on the planet. If a cat's coat were detachable, it would toss it to you without looking at you each time it walked into the room. And you would gratefully take it.

Coolness—Cats are James Dean (dogs are Tom Hanks). Cats are blues and jazz (dogs are country and classic rock). Cats prowl the midnight

hour (dogs chase a ball at three in the afternoon). Cats purr (dogs lick your face). Everything cats do is cool. That's why the expression "cool cat" exists and the expression "cool wombat" does not. Want to create the world's coolest cartoon dude for the front of a Cheetos bag? Better make him a cat. What's cooler than a cat wearing sunglasses?

Sleekness—The design of a cat is all elegant lines. The movement of a cat is slinky. The sound of a cat is silence. And you know that thing high fashion models walk on? There's a reason it's called a catwalk, not a hippo-stomp, a kangaroo-hop, or a warthog-lumber. Humans long to be as sleek and graceful as cats.

Aloofness—Call them detached, call them reserved, call them snobbish, call them haughty, but one thing's for certain: cats don't give a litter box Lincoln Log what the mortals in the room think about them. That's cattitude.

Confidence—A cat can manage to look casual and self-assured while strolling along a tightwire over the Grand Canyon. A cat will fling itself into space, do a somersault in the air, land on a surface the size of a dime, and look at you like, "What?!" Most of all, a cat will assume you want to love it whenever it deigns to bestow a crumb of attention on you. Why? Confidence.

Mystery—A dog wears its heart on its face; a cat keeps its heart in a little leather carrying case stashed in its fur. It will let you know what it is thinking and feeling *if and when* it is good and ready to do so. Meanwhile, you will receive your orders on a need-to-know basis. And you happily accept this role.

Smarts—Scientists claim that only humans are capable of abstract thought and planning. Scientists, evidently, have not watched a cat turn a doorknob with its paws, figure out your plans to give it medicine before you've even lifted your butt off the couch, or map out a strategy for jumping to the place where the human has stored the cream.

Unpredictability—This is perhaps the most distinctive element of Cattitude. A cat can change from superior to silly, cool to cuddly, mysterious to mushy at the drop of a ball of yarn, and will soften the defenses of even the most hardened DICK (um, maybe we ought to rephrase that).

The point is, Cattitude is totally under the cat's control. Cats turn it on and off as needed in order to more skillfully bend humans to their will. The unwitting two-leggeds do their part by not requiring a whole lot of skill in order to be bent. In fact, Catakists *want* to be put under the spell of Cat.

That's the fascinating thing about cat worshipers: they *choose* to be put in a submissive position to Cat. There is no law requiring people to have cats. No, people go out and proactively acquire felines, shelling out top dollar to do so, knowing full well that they are entering a lifelong subservient relationship.

Why? They are under the spell of cattitude.

II. Cattitude in Action

Virtually everything a cat does—from the way it sits in front of your computer monitor staring at you for no apparent reason to the way it converts the highest piece of furniture in every room into Pride Rock to the way it lifts its ears in a little V of disdain whenever you create so much as a decibel of sound in its general vicinity—drips with Cattitude. Here are a few practices that truly embody and exemplify Cattitude:

"That was intentional." Cats pioneered the concept of "I meant to do that," which humans immediately seized upon and have tried to emulate ever since. A cat never makes a mistake. When Cat miscalculates

the propulsion and trajectory necessary to successfully land its jump on the intended target, or mistakes its own tail for a small mammal, it simply looks at you as if to say, "Excellent. That confirms my hypothesis that *that* action is pointless."

"*I* say which water I drink." Few cats in recorded history have sipped water from a dish a human has offered. Rather, it will drink from the dripping faucet, the "throne," the decorative fountain, the fish tank, and most often from the drinking cup the human has just set down on her desk.

"Hands where I can see them and step away from the chow." Cat will literally bite the hand that feeds it. The instant you set food down for a cat, it gives you the stink eye, like a leopard at the watering hole seeing you as its jungle competition.

"Which is more important, me or a stupid piece of paper?" Cats, as everyone knows, don't come when called. That's for dogs. The only known way to get a cat to "come" and "sit" is focus your attention on any type of paperwork: pay some bills or start reading a book, magazine, or newspaper. The cat will instantly materialize out of nowhere and insert itself between you and the object of your attention, as if to say, "I'm what you really want to look at."

"Just passing through." Cats will repeatedly walk past humans going in the same direction, without ever going back the other way. They will do this until the human takes notice. The purpose of this behavior? To short-circuit your mind. Why? Because Cat can.

III. Cattitude Sells

The greatest proof of how effective Cattitude is at bending the human will is the use of cats in branding. Humans put their bucks where their beliefs are, and humans clearly believe in Cat. If advertisers want a product to be seen as cool, sexy, powerful, dominant, confident, athletic, or sleek, it pairs the product with a cat. If they want the product to be seen as cute, cuddly, warm, or fuzzy, the product is paired with a kitten. Perhaps that's why the images of cats, large and small, are used to sell everything from movie studios to Japanese junk food, from breakfast cereal to running shoes, and from fireworks to cheese curls.

In short, every single thing a person could want.

Cattitude in the Stadium

One industry in particular has made a killing from Cattitude: professional sports. MLB has the Tigers, the NHL has the Panthers. And without being able to rely on cat names—such as lions, jaguars, panthers, and bengals—the NFL would have gone bankrupt two decades ago, having been forced to settle for team names like: *The Detroit Deer*, *The Jacksonville Jellyfish*, or *The Cincinnati Chipmunks*.

Collegiate sports are even more cat-crazy. Looking only at four-year colleges with Division I teams, there are no fewer than forty-six teams called the Tigers, thirty-three named the Panthers, twenty-seven called the Cougars, thirty-two teams named the lions, and twenty-seven teams named the Wildcats. Cat mascots impart toughness, agility, and speed to athletes. With a cat name, your team exudes cattitude!

Cattitude on the Road

The industry that has truly made Cattitude its bread and butter is the auto industry. Carmakers want their products to be associated with *all* the attributes of Cattitude: pride, sexiness, power, confidence. Cars pine to be feline. In fact, they should just apply for recognition by the CFA (Cat Fanciers Association) as an official breed of cat and get it over with.

Not only can you put a tiger in your tank and a purr in your engine, but you can proudly drive a car with the name of virtually any cat you choose.

Just a sampling of those that have been offered:

- Jaguar
- Mercury Cougar
- Lamborghini Cheetah
- Buick Wildcat
- Sunbeam Tiger
- Mercury Lynx
- Dodge Challenger Hellcat
- Ford Puma
- Mercury Bobcat
- Geely Beauty Leopard (China)
- MDI Mini-Cat (France)
- Isuzu Leopard (China)
- Reliant Kitten

IV. At Their Beck and Claw: Our Attitude Toward Cattitude

Cattitude has had its influence on every aspect of human culture. Cats hypnotize us into viewing them in a positive light, despite the fact that they provide us no services and treat us with thinly disguised (or maybe not disguised at all) disdain much of the time. For some reason, we seem to like it when cats do this. Dogs, on the other hand, work their furry butts off for us as service dogs, guardians, and rescuers, then greet us at the end of the day with bright eyes, wet kisses, and wagging tails. Yet dogs are often punished for many behaviors we accept as normal for cats: biting, scratching, destroying things, making noise.

The way we elevate cats and, um, throw dogs to the hounds is even reflected in our language. Notice how most dog-related expressions have a negative connotation . . .

- in the doghouse
- gone to the dogs
- dogging it
- the dog days
- sick as a dog
- dirty dog
- lie down with dogs, wake up with fleas
- meaner than a junkyard dog

. . . while cat-related expressions are quite complimentary and positive, or at least reflect Cat's superiority over humans . . .

- the cat's meow
- purring like a kitten
- the cat's pajamas
- cool cat
- catnap
- the cat's whiskers
- fat cat
- let sleeping cats lie
- sitting in the catbird seat
- to bell a cat

The most telling example is when we use the word *dog* or *cat* itself to describe a human.

A **dog** is an ugly word for someone who may not necessarily fit into society's definition of beautiful. (People who use the word dog to describe a human are pigs and jackasses, two other animals used to describe someone in a derogatory manner, when the animals themselves are well above the actions perpetrated by those we call by those names.)

A **cat** is a cool word for a cool person. To call someone a cat is to acknowledge their basic chillness and sense of style. A human cat is urban, sophisticated, hip, musical. A human cat wears shades. A human cat plays sax, guitar, or bass. A human cat does not wear high-waisted Bermuda shorts and eat at Golden Corral.

V. Surrender to Purr-fection: The Sacred Attributes of Cat

Cattitude, in the common use of the word, refers to the cold shoulder that cats give the rest of the animal kingdom, including Man, based on Cat's natural superiority and entitlement. But in the world of Catakism, the word has broader applications. It refers to all the unique traits that cats possess, not just their most condescending ones.

Cat boasts many mystical qualities that render her objectively superior to Man on a spiritual, physical, and mental level. Though DICKs deny many of these feline qualities, Catakists celebrate and honor them.

These traits are known in the catma of Catakism as the Nine Sacred Attributes of Cat.

The Nine Sacred Attributes

1. Cats can teleport. Cats possess the ability to dematerialize and reappear within locked cabinets, under platform beds with no entry points, and from behind closed doors. More baffling than the question of *how* cats teleport is the question of *why*. For Cat *never* teleports to a place that serves its purposes. One would think that given her abilities, Cat would beam herself to the middle of a bird cage or inside the fridge, where the tuna casserole resides, but no. The cat teleports itself to places such as the inside of your grandfather's ventriloquist trunk, which hasn't been opened since Grandpa shuffled off to that great *America's Got Talent* audition in the sky, and then yowls at you as if you were personally responsible for placing her there.

Why do cats do this? Presumably to advance their ultimate mission on Earth: to destroy human reason and replace it with sound effects from old *Tom and Jerry* cartoons.

2. Cats are Zen masters. Cats are so chill, so Zen, so Eckhart Tolle, they make a sloth look like a drive-time DJ on a Red Bull jag. Cats are so adept at living in the present moment—just witness a cat watching a mouse hole—that time literally does not exist for them, until a human comes plodding along hitting a spoon on a dish and shouting, "Time for din-din, Tiddlywinks!"

Cats are so Zen that they literally subtract stress from humans. A cat can lower human blood pressure just by lying on the human's lap (fact).

3. Cats commune with the spirit world. Cats have a tough job to do. Not only do they need to give *us* the cold shoulder 24/7, but they also need to give the cold shoulder to the vast array of ghosts and disembodied spirits *they* can see but we can't. There is no doubt that cats can see ghosts—their eyes often focus on the exact spot in space where a nonbeing is passing by.

The ability to see ghosts also explains why every now and then, without warning, a cat leaps up into the air as if someone had just tried to give it an uninvited rectal exam and runs out of the room screeching.

4. Cats are ninjas. Cat possesses a fine-tuned athletic ability that surpasses that of an Olympic gymnast and ballet dancer combined. Try this experiment. Gently slide your hands under a sleeping cat. Now, with no warning whatsoever, and all the stealth you can muster, toss that sleeping cat into the air—definitely a DICK move. Watch as the cat quickly goes through the following progression:

1. awaken
2. analyze the current in-flight situation

3. realease a nails-on-the-blackboard screech
4. wheel about in the air to hiss at you
5. arch her back and do a backflip in midair
6. hit the ground, sticking the landing with all four paws
7. return to her previous location
8. lick herself
9. go back to sleep

What if a human—say, you—faced a similar scenario. Imagine some-one placing your sleeping body in a catapult and pulling the lever. If you are like most two-leggeds, you will go through the following pro-gression:

1. whiz through air
2. strike wall surface
3. get fitted for full-body cast

5. Cats are psychic. Everyone who lives with a cat knows that felines are psychic. Unfortunately, cats expend 98 percent of their psychic powers not on solving crimes, warning humanity about upcoming di-sasters, finding lost children, or helping their humans win lotteries, but on jumping onto their human's lap the instant they decide to go to the toilet. Without fail, the moment a cat owner has the idea, "Think I'll pee before my bladder explodes," a cat comes hurtling in from out of nowhere, curls up on her lap, and instantly goes to sleep. Why? No one knows. Perhaps to remind the human how futile his personal agendas are.

The other area where Cat's psychic powers become evident is around veterinary appointments. Cat unerringly knows when vet ap-pointments are scheduled, even if the human says nothing about it. Approximately nine minutes before departure time, Cat will exercise yet another of its sacred attributes . . . read on.

6. Cats can disappear. Cats vanish into thin air in advance of the following events: veterinary appointments, groomer appointments, the administration of medicine, claw trimming time, and the arrival of your cousins from Duluth with the *adorable* toddlers.

Cats can also reappear, seemingly from out of nowhere.

7. Cats can implement the Feline Mind Meld. Every cat is capable of putting human beings under its spell through use of the Feline Mind Meld. The cat simply stares into the human's eyes for fifteen seconds, with occasional slow blinks, and the human becomes incapable of any behavior that does not serve the cat. This state of hypnosis can be so extreme that victims have been found wandering the aisles of the nearest Purr-Babies-R-Us, holding twenty-pound bags of freeze-dried chicken breast treats, with no idea how they got there. Clear case of falling prey to the Feline Mind Meld.

8. Cats can liquefy. Cats possess the astonishing ability to instantly transform from vertebrate to invertebrate. They can dissolve their skeletons at will and turn into a warm puddle of purring fur under two conditions: (1) the stroking and patting of a skilled human hand, or (2) the desire to pass through an opening way too small for their bodies, such as the quarter-inch space between the bottom of the door and the floor, thus explaining their ability to appear virtually anywhere.

9. Cats have nine lives. Perhaps the best known of the sacred attributes is Cat's fine-tuned ability to reincarnate. Humans are in such awe of this feline ability that they decided to mimic it with the invention of multiple lives in video games, which led to the growth of the worldwide video game industry, which led to an increase in video game programmers and designers, which led to the establishment of Cat as the number one pet on the planet. Why? Because all individuals working in any aspect of the software industry are required by law to possess a cat.

VI. Purr-sonality

Cattitude reveals itself in all felines, from the hairless Sphinx kitten with the kite-sized ears to the mighty lion. Whereas there is virtually no similarity between, say, a hummingbird and an ostrich, even though both are birds, every member of the feline family exudes *cat* in everything it does.

Yet under the umbrella of Cattitude, kitties can have remarkably varied purr-sonalities. Catakists throughout the ages have *cat*-alogued a number of distinct purr-sonalities amongst the felines that have graced their homes. Each purr-sonality is deemed worthy of worship in its own right.

The Shadow—This cat chooses a single human to Velcro itself to night and day. When the human cooks a meal, the cat "helps." When the human sleeps, the cat curls up on its pillow. All day, every day, the cat does every single thing the human does, and yet the cat manages to make it appear that every decision was *his* idea and that your schedules just *happen* to overlap by coincidence. All Catakists secretly crave a Shadow cat.

The Talker—This kitty carries on a nonstop commentary about everything that's going on in his life, from his backyard hunting prospects to the local mating scene. From the continually plaintive yowling sound in the Talker's voice, one can assume that things aren't going too great in kitty world, but one doesn't *have* to assume. Just ask him—he'll be happy to explain.

The Freakazoid—This kitty is never quite at home in our humdrum plane of existence and spends her days interacting with aliens from another dimension. Her eyes are always wide open, her head constantly darting from place to place as she stalks and jumps on invisible (to us) aliens, fiercely tackling them and cute-ing them into submission.

The Sun God—Unlike the average cat, which spends 17.5 hours a day napping, the Sun God spends most of it asleep in the beam of sunlight coming in the living room window. As the beam travels across the room with the moving sun, he remains within the beam, yet you never actually see him move. Beam me up, Scottish Fold!

The Total Cuddle Muffin—This rare creature, highly welcomed by Catakists, spends her entire life span in a single environment: the human lap. When not napping, she is purring and/or receiving chin rubs, cheek rubs, head rubs, and belly rubs, while the human expresses gratitude for the opportunity to be of service.

The Drill Sergeant—This kitty is the self-appointed keeper of order in the human household. She keeps track of the humans' schedules with a stern eye and ensures that everyone is on task by issuing a lethal glare to all who stray from the path. If there are dogs in the household, the Drill Sergeant keeps a vigilant eye on them with a slightly raised paw, ready to whack them into order whenever they do anything, well, dog-like. All dogs recognize the Drill Sergeant as the alpha in the house. As do all humans.

The Great White (and Black) Hunter—On the plus side, this kitty actually earns her keep. On the negative side, she does so by patrolling your house and yard, rooting out creatures that you would prefer not to know even existed, such as rats, mice, snakes, moles, voles, millipedes, and the occasional scorpion. At the end of the day, the hunter dutifully turns in her pelts and skins—with a little bit of fresh pancreas attached—and awaits her reward from you.

Jacques Pussteau—This kitty explorer spends his life uncovering the mysteries of science, from the properties of spilled water to the way various objects respond to the Law of Gravity. They say curiosity killed the cat, but any human who shares its home with Jacques Pussteau knows that curiosity may kill the cat *owner*.

The A-hole—There's no nice way to say it: some kitties are just tiny feline a-holes: grumpy, surly, aggressive, unpleasant, and rude. The Catakist fortunate enough to land an A-hole for a "pet" gets to groom, feed, stroke, spoil, praise, and pander to his cat 24/7 and in return is scratched, swatted, bitten, hissed at, and haughtily ignored. Yet the true Catakist feels honored by her cat's presence.

It's impossible to know what purr-sonality your adult cat is going to end up with, because kittens have yet to fully develop their purr-sonality and are all considered freakin' adorable. But one thing is for certain: your cat will be sure to have the one purr-sonality you feel least equipped to deal with. This is Cat's way of helping humans grow, adapt, and evolve to their highest potential.

Ninefold Path Guidepost #4

When encountering a feline exuding cattitude,
bow down and become its servant for life . . .
and be damn happy to do so.

Human beings the world over proclaim freedom and self-determination to be the highest of human values. Then they go out and get a cat. A human who lives with a cat immediately enters a relationship of indentured servitude. His entire life revolves around making his cat master comfortable and happy, while deferring fulfillment of his own needs.

THE BOOK OF CAT POSTS

An exploration of purr-aphernalia

I. Temples of Cat Worship

Most religions are practiced in places specially built for worship, such as churches, mosques, temples, or, in some cases, man caves, stadiums, and malls. Not so in Catakism. The reason there are no formal temples of Catakism is that this would require practitioners to go to a separate place to express their devotion, and this wouldn't fly unless Cat could attend as well. And so, Catakists turn their homes, offices, and automobiles into temples to Cat, filling them with signs and symbols of our devotion.

Generally speaking, the more outward signs of their belief a human displays, the more dedicated that believer is. For instance, a casual yoga enthusiast buys a mat and a pair of yoga pants, tops it with a tank top and pops into the studio once or twice a week. A yoga *devotee* owns no less than three mats, has the om symbol tattooed on her shoulder, replaces her lawn with a Zen garden, and spends hours a day in lotus pose.

Likewise, you can easily tell the degree of a Catakist's devotion by the sheer quantity of cat-themed artifacts that surrounds them.

Come near the home of a devout Catakist and here's what you might see:

- a barrage of *Cat Xing, Beware: Attack Cat*, and *Cats at Play* safety signs lining the walkway, which, of course, is constructed with paw-shaped flagstones
- a jack-o'-lantern carved to create a cat's face
- a snow kitty in the yard (no anthropocentric snow*men* for this family)
- a sleeping cat key-hiding statue in the garden
- a cat-themed welcome mat proclaiming *Wipe Your Paws, All Visitors Must Be Approved by Cat*, and *Cats Welcome, People Tolerated*

All this before you've gotten in the door. Once you step inside this Cat Chapel, your eyes will alight on:

- a refrigerator covered in cat magnets holding up pictures of, you guessed it, cats
- a cat wall clock complete with synchronized swinging tail and moving eyes
- a cat butt pencil sharpener
- a cat-giving-birth tissue dispenser (yes, these exist and don't ask where the tissues come out)
- a Chia cat
- a coffee mug that proclaims, "I was normal about three cats ago"
- a cat calendar in every room
- et *catera, et catera*

The sheer number of kitty-themed objects and artwork—known as *purr-aphernalia*—with which Catakists surround themselves is a pretty accurate measure of their degree of fanaticism. In even the most casual Catakist's home, you cannot swing a cat by the tail (nor would you do so under penalty of death) without striking two dozen articles of religious purr-aphernalia.

II. Cat-egories of Purr-aphernalia

So much cat-themed ~~crap junk doodoo~~ merchandise has been created throughout history, it is enough to fill every house on Earth from floor to ceiling an estimated seventeen times over. From cat snowglobes to kitty neckties to cat-themed caskets (yes) to guitars with cat-shaped sound holes, there is seemingly not a single object on Earth that cannot be—and has not *been*—manufactured in a cat-themed version. Grumpy Cat driveway sealant! Mr. Whiskers mortuary equipment! Hello Kitty grenade launchers! Felix the cathode-ray tube!

If you go to a certain popular merchandise website (okay, it's Zazzle) and type the word "cats" in the search box, you will get more than 1.7 million product results, at last count (fact). Cat products can be found in the clothing, home and pets, electronics, office products, and art departments, and even the craft supplies section. And that's just on one website! (Got my eye on a "Cat Daddy" T-shirt.)

Purr-aphernalia is used to demonstrate Catakists' faith in two essential ways: by kittifying the world of humans, and by humanizing the world of cats

In both ways, Catakism seeks to bring the human and feline worlds closer together. Because Catakists can't stand the fact that nature was so cruel as to make them two separate species.

The sheer overwhelming amount of purr-aphernalia available in the world makes it necessary to cat-egorize it into classes.

While much of this merchandise might seem like junk to a casual observer, for Catakists purr-aphernalia represents the objects of their faith, much like a crucifix, a menorah, or a Buddha statue.

Liturgical Calendars (i.e., Cat Calendars)

Every Catakist's household contains multiple calendars to keep track of the liturgical year (National Cat Day, birthdays of all feline friends, etc.). And every one of them features images of cats. If you have a Catakist on your holiday gift list, your default gift is a cat calendar. Fortunately, you don't have to worry if she already has one. She does, and she's more than happy to hang up another. For a calendar is no longer a tool for keeping track of the days and months of the year—we don't need those anymore; we have smartphones—it is a tool for measuring how long one must wait before flipping to a new cat picture.

Liturgical (cat) calendars exist in a nearly infinite variety, like:

Things that come in twelves. Twelve angry cats, twelve signs of the zodi-cat, the twelve days of Cat-mas, you get the idea.

Kitty in a . . . cup or box, or cats in hats.

Breed-specific, and no breed of cat is left out, picture the famous Nude Kitty Calendar, featuring the hairless Sphinx cat in poses that, once glimpsed, cannot be unseen.

Cats dressed as movie stars, athletes, and historical figures. Na-paw-leon, anyone? Diane Kitten? Jack Nick-claws? Tiger Woods (nah, too easy)?

Then, of course, there are calendars of cats being sad, cats being naughty, cats at work, cats at play, fat cats, skinny cats, cats napping, cats looking wise, cats acting silly, cats looking surprised, cats looking indifferent.

In other words, take twelve random photos of cats, Photoshop them onto a generic calendar, and give it to a Catakist. Boom, perfect gift.

Felinical Chalices and Urns (Cat Mugs)

There is a mystical connection between the love of hot beverages and the love of cats. Every temple of Catakism has a cabinet full of cat-themed mugs. Some may be cat-shaped, some might feature photos of the human's real-life kitties, and some will feature sayings, such as:

- Coffee Meow
- Kit-Tea Cat
- Best Cat Mom
- My Kids Have Paws
- Cat-feinated

- 🐾 Because Cat
- 🐾 Cat Dander Is a Condiment

Still not sure if you're a Catakist? Observe the cup you're currently drinking from. If it features a cat face, wonder no more.

Scrolls of Wisdom (Cat Posters)

These scrolls contain snippets of wisdom, or Catma, that the faithful use to get through their day and keep the faith.

The poster business would have gone belly-up after Farrah Fawcett decided to cut her hair in 1981 were it not for cats. Who among you has not owned a poster that features a dangling cat urging you to "Hang In There!"? Fortunately for the poster industry, Catakists purchase these scrolls and use them like wallpaper in their homes, offices, gym lockers, and Winnebagos.

As with mugs and calendars, cat posters come in an infinite variety, but just a few of the obligatory cat-egories are:

Posters of "cat thoughts"—With gems like: "Get yourself a pet human, they said; it'll be fun, they said." Or, "I didn't gain weight, the box shrunk."

Cat lists—These include lists of cats' house rules, cats' suggestions for world peace, and cats' Ten Commandments—and perhaps should also include cats' top ten ways to get humans to stop making cat lists.

French cat poster art—Catakism, or *Chatachisme*, as it is known in Paris, has been alive and well in France for centuries, as evidenced by the never-ending stream of antique-looking French cat-themed advertising posters that populate gift shops. These posters, with titles such as *"Chat Noir,"* *"Trois Chats,"* and *"Le Chat Domestique,"* allow the buyer to pretend that there is a sophisticated, continental aspect to their kitty obsession. Cats, for their part, love seeing French poster art on the wall, because it signals to them that this is a human from whom they can demand crème fraîche, escargots, beurre blanc, and Brie cheese.

New Yorker **cat covers**—Has there ever been a cover of *New Yorker* magazine that did not feature a cat? Oh yes, there was the one with the kittens. And then there was the other one that showed only a cat's *shadow*. A *New Yorker* cover on your wall gives you the pretentiousness-cred of being a *New Yorker* reader without the actual work of reading the magazine.

Cats Making Weird Faces—These close-ups are usually accompanied with one-word captions, such as Chillin', Busted, Awesome, and Dude.

Cat Mockery and Belittlement—There is also a strange subset of cat posters dedicated to showing fat cats stuck in small objects, cats with cans stuck to their heads, cat faces grafted onto absurd objects, and cats wearing ridiculous things on their heads. These represent the dark side of Catakism: those "believers" who gain a sense of superiority by mocking the very thing they revere. They are the equivalent of the "rich guy slipping on a banana peel" scene in films that kept the working class happily toiling away for much of the twentieth century.

Sacred Vestments (Cat T-Shirts and Pajamas)

Catakists wear kitty T-shirts and pajamas to proudly proclaim their Catakistic faith. Practically speaking, however, cat T-shirts function as an early warning system. They announce to would-be lovers, friends, employers, neighbors, and landlords, "Alert! Alert! This article of clothing contains a certified (and certifiable) cat fanatic. Consider yourself duly warned."

Just a small sampling of the 9.4 trillion choices of cat sayings available on vestments of Catakism through a popular online cat-alog:

- Sorry, I Was Thinking About Cats
- Wanted, Dead *and* Alive: Schrodinger's Cat
- My Other Shirt Is Also Covered in Cat Hair
- Meowy Christmas
- You Say "Crazy Cat Lady" Like It's a Bad Thing
- Professional Cat Herder
- Real Men Love Cats
- It's Not Drinking Alone if the Cat Is Home
- Show Me Your Kitties
- Crazy Cat Lady in Training
- You've Cat to Be Kitten Me Right Meow
- Check Meowt
- All of My Children Have Paws
- Cats Are Like Potato Chips; You Can't Have Just One
- I Work Hard So My Cat Can Have a Better Life
- When I Want Your Opinion I'll Pee on Something (Signed, Cat)
- Cat Hair Is a Décor Choice
- If You Don't Talk to Your Cat About Catnip, Someone Else Will

The above represent Catakistic attempts to kittify the human world, but Catakism also attempts to humanize the feline world. One might say that Man makes Cat in his image and likeness. Just as many faiths encourage believers to make "offerings" to their deities of things that *humans* use and love—water, incense, flowers, fruit, etc.—so does Catakism make useless human offerings to Cat.

Here are some of the standard pieces of purr-aphernalia used to humanize the world of cats:

Idols and Fetishes (Cat Toys)

Catakists identify so strongly with their cats, they imagine cats have the same needs as humans. Even when it comes to entertainment. Cats, however, are self-sufficient entertainment-wise. Remember, they only have to fill about three and a half hours of free time every day. The rest of the time they are napping, eating, and barfing up hair balls. And when they *do* require stimulation of some kind, they are perfectly capable of providing it for themselves. They watch birds in the window, they hunt for mice, they torment the dog.

In other words, they do cat things.

However, many Catakists feel compelled to insert themselves into the cat's natural processes. Thus, they purchase an endless array of cat toys, most of which are designed more for human entertainment. (No self-respecting cat would attach a stuffed mouse to a string; no chase equals no thrill.) Then they anxiously watch to see Mitten's look of wonder and delight when said toy is presented.

In those rare instances when Cat deigns to give the object a moment of fleeting attention, the Catakist is filled with joy. Not because Cat has finally been rescued from the depths of boredom, but because the human has finally registered a blip on Cat's awareness radar, which makes the human feel warm and fuzzy, right?

Here are just some of the *cat* toys Catakists fill their homes with:

Confuse-a-Cat toys. There is an endless inventory of "toys" designed to confuse and "stimulate" kitties by presenting them with mazes, puzzles, and hidden objects. Why we think cats enjoy having their minds scrambled is uncertain, but *we* certainly love to watch kitties interact with:

Whack-a-mouse-type games, where cartoonish mice, fish, birds, and frogs appear from random holes. Cats engage with these toys for a short while, until they figure out the hidden order beneath the apparent randomness. Humans, too stupid to see the hidden order, become mystified as to why their cats lose interest so quickly.

Holey boxes (boxes full of holes) from which objects of supposed feline interest are stashed. When cats realize how much work is involved in retrieving objects of dubious value, they revert to the much more fun and less challenging game of tricking humans into giving them everything *they* really want.

Hide-the-food mazes force Cat to solve puzzles in order to eat. Because nothing makes a cat feel loved like making it slave for every tiny morsel of food. Humans love watching cats play with confusing toys, not because the cat is being stimulated, but because the human gets to feel superior to the cat, if only for a brief, fleeting moment.

Electronic prey. Humans spend large amounts of money on electronic gadgets designed to emulate the movement of "wild" prey for cats. These come in the form of mice that run around on tracks, mice that run around loose in the house, fake fish tanks, and fake butterfly gardens. However, kitty prefers chasing the real prey you wish didn't live in your home.

Jingly balls. Look in any direction in a cat owner's home and you will see plastic jingly balls strewn across the floor. What you will never see is a cat playing with a jingly ball. Some scientists believe jingly balls have evolved to the point where they have gained the ability to reproduce.

Catnip-filled things. Catnip is kitty crack. Nature gave this little gift to kitty, and humans can take no credit for it other than serving as Cat's dealer.

Laser pointers. Like catnip, the red laser light has an effect on Cat's brain that is neurological and out of human control. Like a human who is exposed to porn, once a kitty is exposed to the red laser light, there's no going back. Humans cherish the feeling of control it gives them over their cats. (After all, cats control humans most of the time.) That feeling soon vanishes, however, when the human realizes he is just as addicted to watching kitty chase the dot as kitty is to chasing the dot. A bad idea for both species.

Plush toys fail spectacularly because cats have zero interest in soft stuffed things that just sit there and smell like polyester—replace the stuffing with catnip, and once again you have their interest.

Random trash. Eventually the human learns that Cat will contentedly play with the wrappers, bags, and boxes that toys come in, as well as cellophane, balls of foil, scraps of wrapping paper, ribbons, bows, and packing peanuts.

Things on wands. Get a wand. Stick something on the end of it. Boom, cat toy.

Thrones and Pedestals (Cat Furniture and Equipment)

The difference between a Cat-akist and a *normal* cat owner (if such a being exists) is that normal cat owners think all that's required to own a cat is a simple litter box, some feeding dish-es, and a scratching post or two. Catakism practitioners know that if you're not spending 92 percent of your disposable income on your cat, you're not trying hard enough. And one of the best ways to burn off some of that irksome extra cash is specialized kitty furniture and equipment.

It is the sheer quantity and creativity of cat furniture that really distinguishes a Catakism temple from a novice cat home. Walking into a Catakism temple is akin to going inside the mind of Dr. Seuss. There are tim-tumblers and zam-zankas, blam-zookas and ta-twinklers, but nothing vaguely resembling a chair that a human can sit upon.

Some of the obligatory furnishings a temple must contain:

Luxury litter boxes—Several models of unnecessarily elegant and complex litter boxes are available to the discerning cat steward, starting with the wood-paneled free-standing model with slide-out litter drawer and progressing all the way to the ultimate self-cleaning model that is hooked up to the plumbing system and has more complicated physics than the Large Hadron Collider.

Scratching posts—Designed to give kitty something to sharpen its claws on, thus preserving the human's furniture. Every true

Catakist, however, also learns the Law of the Scratching Post, which is: the odds of your cat using the scratching post rather than the upholstered chair right next to it are inversely proportional to the cost of the chair. Catakists get around this problem by eliminating human furniture entirely. A Catakism temple is a veritable forest of scratching posts in every height, width, color, and texture. Alas, the only household member who uses the posts for actual scratching is weird Aunt Meryl with the chafing issue.

Cat trees—These include all of the carpet-covered climbing structures of infinite complexity available to the cat owner eager to put his wallet on a weight-loss program. Cat trees are essentially altars to Cat. Thrones. Pedestals. Each one contains multiple platforms for easy worshipping. To a Catakist, the elaborateness of a home's cat tree network is a measure of the degree of love and devotion she has for her kitty. For Cat, it is a measure of the degree of submission of the resident humans. When a cat tree evolves to the point of having central air conditioning, remotely controlled lighting, and automatic treat dispensers, it is elevated to the status of cat condo.

Tunnels—The average Catakist's home has more miles of tunnel than a drug lord's basement. Cat tunnels come in all hideous colors and can be free-standing, attached to cat trees, or built into human furniture and walls. Tunnels can also occur naturally as a result of a cat's attempt to burrow out of a home in which a student violinist resides. To a human, a cat tunnel represents the sacred honoring of a cat's primal secretive nature. To Cat, a tunnel represents a place to hide in order to whack the ass of a passing dog.

Cubbies, beds, and sleepy holes—Because cats nap approximately 17.5 hours a day, and in complete comfort on any available surface, Catakists naturally feel kitties need a variety of options for sleeping on. Some are meant to be slept *on*, yet Cat will sleep *under* them; some are meant to be slept *under*, so Cat will naturally choose to sleep *on top of* them; and others are meant to be slept *inside of*, thus you will most likely find Precious belly up *beside* them. After lining every available horizontal surface in the house with sleep-inducing items, Catakists can be heard exclaiming, "Look at you, Tinkerbell, all you do is sleep all day!"

Cat walkways, bridges, and trapezes—No Catakist home would be complete without a vast, interconnected system of elevated paths, bridges, and walkways designed so that Cat never has to sully herself by setting a paw on a floor covered in jingly balls.

Cat "strolling environments"—Catakists like to take their kitties for walks in strollers. Unfortunately, the open design of a standard stroller won't work with cats, who jump out at the first street corner, head to the nearest barn, and start a family. Therefore, cat strollers are designed as rolling mini Shawshanks, keeping your kitty locked in, while *you* get the benefits of a walk. Because there's nothing Cat loves more than being stuck in a small, inescapable space and shown a world of wildlife with which it can't interact.

Cat wheels—Most forms of exercise are impractical for cats—jogging, weightlifting, Zumba. So dedicated Catakists often purchase giant hamster wheels for their kitties. Cats use exercise machines precisely the way cat owners do—once. The machine then becomes a four-foot-high, two-hundred-dollar clothes hanger much like your NordicTrack®.

And that barely *scratches* the surface of the purr-aphernalia found in temples of Catakism. Don't forget waving-cat statues, cat angels, cat wrapping paper, cat throw pillows, Cat-opoly board game, cat iPhone covers, cat lamps, humorous cat trophies, etc.

If you're a Catakist, you haven't.

Ninefold Path Guidepost #5

If there is room in your home for the humans to eat, relax, and procreate, you don't own enough cat equipment. Buy more.

Whose house is this anyway, yours or the cat's? If you even have to paws to think about this, you are not a true Catakist. If you do know the correct answer—i.e., the cat's—then why are you wasting time shopping for new end tables when they really need to be replaced by cat trees anyway?

THE BOOK OF PURRS

The purr-fect conversation

I. The Sacred Purr

All Catakists know that Cat is the most enlightened being on Earth, but they don't necessarily know why. Here we must turn toward Eastern Catakism for the answer. The reason cats are so Zen is that they are born knowing a sacred mantra—the purr—which they recite many times daily.

When listened to carefully, the purr is almost the exact same sound a Nepalese monk makes when chanting the sacred om (seriously, give those monks a listen). Cat, like the monk, uses this sound to enter a state of profound peace and meditation.

How is it that a cat can get zero exercise, lie around all day, and yet fly into action like a finely tuned ninja at an instant's notice? The purr. The purr is what keeps the kitty in the zone 24/7.

Here's what humans don't understand. Humans think the purr is a *sign* of inner peace. To Cat, though, the purr is a *vehicle* it uses to *achieve* inner peace. Therefore, the more stressful its environment, the more frantically the cat needs to purr in order to find peace. That is why cats often purr around humans.

The cat, you see, is never sure when the human is going to suddenly seize it under the front legs, dangle it in the air, and say, "Who's the cutest squishy-squashums in the whole wide world?" in a voice so high pitched that it shatters the kitty's Wedgewood crystal dining chalice.

Cat must keep herself in a constant state of physical and spiritual preparedness. And that is the purr-pose of the low rumble.

II. Prayer (Talking to Cats)

The thing that Catakists do that most distinguishes them as cat worshippers is talk to their cats. Cat-talk, in fact, can be regarded as the chief form of prayer in Catakism.

Believers converse with their kitties nonstop. From morning till night, and then in their dreams. Cat talk—like much religious prayer—is driven by our need for constant reassurance that things are okay between we the lowly human and Cat. So we toss out an endless stream of conversational gems to Tibbles, such as, "Who's a good kitty? Tibbles is a good kitty," "Who's so cute I want to smoosh her to death with hugs and kisses?" and "Who's so freaking adorable I want to roll her up into a rope and whip myself with her till I go insane?" (Catakists often express their uncontainable love for cats in terms that would result in their arrest and/or psychiatric commitment if taken literally.)

The Sermon on the Maytag

As part of their daily prayer, Catakists feel a strong need to narrate their daily activities to Cat . . . "Mommy is putting fabric softener in the machine now. Do you know why? So kitty's blanket will be nice and soft. Now Mommy's closing the lid. Do you know why? So kitty can't fall in. Because Mommy loves kitty. Now Mommy's going to empty the dishwasher. Look! All the people dishes go up there. And all the kitty dishes go down here. Now Mommy's reaching for the vodka. Yes, she is."

Kitty talk is not just a substitute for human talk. Most Catakists, if they're being completely honest, would *rather* talk to cats than humans.

Do cats actually listen to anything humans say to them? Well, that is the subject of great debate, even among Catakists. One thing perhaps everyone can agree on is that cats listen to humans *very selectively*. And most of the time, they select "off" as their default setting. Which is perhaps why humans have such a compulsion to keep the vocal assault going 24/7.

III. The Feline Falsetto Frequency (FFF)

When talking to a cat—i.e., begging for forgiveness, asking what Socks wants for din-din, making a confession, etc.—it is physically impossible for a cat lover not to lapse into a high-pitched, subservient, baby talk voice, much like a schoolteacher would use to plead to her third-grade class to practice their multiplication tables.

This vocal condition is known as the Feline Falsetto Frequency (FFF, or Triple-F). FFF affects approximately 99.8 percent of Catakists, and even some DICKs have been known to be affected when talking to Cat. Triple-F causes the edges of the vocal cords to vibrate involuntarily in the presence of a cat, raising the pitch several octaves higher than the person's normal speaking voice. The cuter the cat, the more immediate and extreme the case of FFF. A kitten with disproportionately large ears and eyes can cause a case of FFF so extreme that the throat of the innocent cat worshipper can  become constricted and the victim may pass out from a lack of oxygen.

Triple-F is nearly always accompanied by a compulsion to use invented words like "smooshums." Science is less certain about why this occurs. Some say it's because we think of kitties as our children and automatically want to talk to them that way. Others suggest it's because we ourselves revert to mental childhood in the presence of the overwhelming cuteness of kitties.

But perhaps the servile, placating, walking-on-eggshells tone humans use with kitties is a reflection of their constant fear that Cat will tire of them and dismiss them with a casual flick of her paw.

Does a cat actually enjoy being spoken to like he's a toddler who has somehow gotten hold of the nuclear codes? The jury is still out on that. Some scientists think cats have a significantly higher range of hearing than humans and do indeed respond better to high-pitched human voices. However, no studies have been conducted on this due to the fact that researchers have been unable to create a control group. That is, no humans can be found who are able to speak to cats in a *normal* voice, even for testing purposes. It's been tried for centuries, and nobody has been able to rise to this seemingly impossible challenge.

Ninefold Path Guidepost #6

When speaking to a cat, employ the Feline Falsetto Frequency under penalty of ex-claw-munication

Constantly speaking in a much-higher-than-normal voice to one's cat reminds believers of the position cats hold in relation to humans: much higher.

IV. Our Prayers Are Answered (Conversations with Cats)

Cats will often engage in two-way conversations with humans, answering each of their questions and responding to each of their statements with a perfectly intoned squeak or meow. Not all kitties *choose* to chat with humans, but some are such great chatters, their agents have received offers for them to host their own late-night variety shows (provided the kitty host could be persuaded to stay in her chair and not run backstage to partake in the delightful selections offered on the craft service table).

So, what's going on here? Is kitty conversation just some form of reflex reaction on the part of cats, as non-cat people suggest? Are cats just messing with us? Those who don't believe cat conversations are real have either never talked to a cat, or never talked to a Catakist. True believers have no doubt whatsoever that they engage in meaningful conversation with their cats. If you plan to challenge them on this, you might want to upgrade your health insurance policy and hire a body-guard.

An unwritten rule of Catakism is that all conversations with kitty must be given priority over human conversations. Over work and so-cial commitments. Over meals. Over household chores. Over romantic relations. Over hobbies and TV shows. Even over conversations with

other kitties. And a kitty conversation, once initiated by either the human or the feline party, is over only when the kitty stops issuing mews, squeaks, and trills. (Warning: if kitty is feeling talkative, this might require canceling your plans for the evening.)

What do cats understand?

Studies are beginning to reveal that cat *owners* actually understand a far larger cat vocabulary than was previously believed, and vice versa (true). Cats may be able to understand not only many human *words*, but also a great many human gestures, intonations, and behaviors. While some Catakists find this research to be exciting, it also represents cause for sobriety. For if cats actually understand what we humans are saying, this has enormous implications for the way we live our lives.

For example:

- If you wish to keep your living room upholstery urine-free and non-shredded, you might not want to say, "I'm thinking about getting a puppy," out loud.
- When you call each one your kitties "the best kitty in the whole world," know that the others are listening and learning that your words can't be trusted. Good luck next time you say, "Come on, try this cat litter, it's the best!"
- If you're a DICK and you never want to see Twinkles again, just cheerfully announce, "I think it might be time to get Twinkles spayed."
- When you come in from grocery shopping, shouting, "I bought the cats the store-brand food 'cause it was cheaper," know that you are igniting a feline hunger strike that could potentially last for months.
- When you give your spouse the ultimatum, "It's me or the cats," realize from that moment forward the cats will be conspiring to make that choice easy for him/her.

Once humans realize how much cats really understand, it changes the fundamental nature of our "cute" and harmless conversations with them. This is even truer when humans understand what cats are really saying back to *them*.

V. The Word of Cat (Cats Talk to Humans)

Science tells us that once cats graduate from kittenhood, they rarely communicate vocally with one another. Cats are vocal *only around humans*. Virtually all of their "speech" is reserved for us. And why do they "speak"? Of course, it's to make humans *do* things for them, such as pet them, feed them, let them in or out, and admire them. In other words, cats use their vocalizations to train humans. This is the profound difference between human-canine talk and human-feline talk. Humans use words to train dogs to do what humans want; cats use words to train humans to do what cats want.

Here are a few examples of *standard* cat vocabulary:

- *Silent mew* = Can you stand how cute I am? Maybe some adoration would be nice right about now.
- *Mew* = Okay, I'm sitting right in front of you, adore me NOW.
- *Meow* = Hello? Am I invisible or what? Get with the adoring, bitch!
- *MEOW* = ADORE ME, HUMAN, OR THERE WILL BE CONSEQUENCES!
- *Mee-ow-www* (with dropping intonation) = Not cool, foolish human, not cool.
- *Myip* = Well, I *never!*
- *Mrrrraaaow* = I'm going to go on Yelp and give this household a crappy review.
- *Mirrrrrow* (in a sing-song tone) = Okay, two-legged interloper, I approve of you, I guess, on a conditional basis, subject to review.

- *Hiss* = You have pissed me off so much I actually think I'm a snake. Come near me and lose a finger.
- *Weird clicking sounds* = Shh, be vewy, vewy quiet, I'm hunting wabbits.

Of course, there are many more. But here's another scientific finding: cats not only have a *general* human "vocabulary," but they also develop a large and unique vocabulary with each human, or group of humans, they are paired with.

Catakists learn to understand and appreciate all the subtleties of their cats' speech. And the more the human understands, the more elaborate kitty's communications become (at least that's what Catakism teaches). A Catakist has no trouble understanding complex messages from kitty such as: "Um, yeah, about the litter box. Seriously?" or "Why are you paying attention to [fill in the blank] when you could be paying attention to ME?"

And some believers claim they can understand even more sophisticated and specific communications such as: "Remember that show we watched together on Animal Planet a few weeks ago? Not the one with the ostriches—that one gave me nightmares—but the one about cultures that worshipped cats? You had a drink, I had one of those freeze-dried chicken hearts. We cuddled. Yeah, can we cue that puppy up again? Glad we have it on-demand."

Whether Catakists can really understand their cats at such a high level of specificity or just need to call in a refill on their medication is not fully known.

VI. Revealing the Mind of Cat (Talking for Cats)

Catakists do more than just *interpret* what they believe their cats are thinking, they put it out there. Whenever they are not talking *to* their cats, they are talking *for* their cats. This is the ultimate way in which Catakists humanize their kitties.

To listen to a Catakist talk for a cat is quite revealing, because 99 percent of the imagined thoughts of the cat revolve around how wonderful, important, and necessary the human is to the cat. For example:

"I wuv you." The number one message we humans imagine cats want to tell us is how much *they* love *us*. Hmm, right. Even odder, this message is often delivered with an Elmer Fudd speech impediment.

"Pick me up, pwease." Catakists have a never-ending itch to pick up their cats. On a subconscious level, though, they know this is annoying and disruptive to the cat, so they pretend the *cat* is asking for it. Again, note the Fudd-like intonation.

"Suitcases make me sad." Whenever Catakists are packing to go on a trip, they imagine the sight of the suitcase breaks the cat's heart. (Of course, the reverse is true. It's the human's heart that is breaking, imagining long days and nights away from kitty.) What the cat may be actually thinking is, "Awesome-looking box filled with black clothes for me to decorate!"

"I'm a bad kitty." When something breaks or spills in the house, humans like to imagine the cat is skulking around with a guilty conscience. The cat's actual attitude is probably more like, "Sh*t happens. Deal with it. Hey, how 'bout giving me a snack? That usually makes you feel better."

VII. The Blessed Intercession of Cat (Talking Through Cats)

Cat is the psychological, spiritual, and emotional center of every temple of Catakism (i.e., household). The humans in the household give so much of their love and attention to the cat that they lose the ability to relate to other human beings in a healthy, human way. All interhuman communication ends up being mediated through the cat, and the humans become unable to communicate with one another when the cat is not present.

Talking *through* the cat is particularly helpful in situations such as:

Icebreaker—Whenever there is awkward silence in the house for any reason, talking to the cat is a surefire way to get past it. Longtime Catakist couples have no idea how to spend time together without the cat, which is why they usually opt for takeout and Netflix rather than an actual date at a restaurant, where they might be forced to talk to *each other* . . . about the cat, of course.

Feline FedEx—Talking to the cat as a means of sending messages to other humans.

> **Example:**
> **Woman to cat:** "Well, Bathsheba, I'm going to the mall if your father wants to come."
> **Man to cat:** "Tell your mother that Daddy would rather chew on his own eyeballs than spend the next two hours hanging around The Furniture Barn with the other husband hostages while your mother ass-tests sofas into the ground."

Woman to cat: "Fine, tell your father that if he doesn't come, he's going to be spending the next two years *sleeping* on that sofa, so he'd better hope Mommy picks a good one."
Man to cat: "Tell your mother I'm getting my ****ing coat."

Kitty Conduit—Another popular reason for talking through cats is to express opinions and render judgments that might be unpopular coming from a human mouth, such as:

- "Look: Kitty doesn't like this sauce—too much salt."
- "Kitty says, 'I can't sleep because the football game is too loud.'"
- "Kitty says, 'I'm ready for Mommy's mommy to go back to Delaware. I want my house back.'"

An alternate way of doing this is to say things to the cat that are really for someone else's ear, like, "Look at you, Mr. Tubs, you're getting so fat, Mommy's starting to wonder if the lady cats find you attractive anymore," or "I like talking to you, Snowball, because you don't interrupt me every five seconds."

VIII. The Gospel of Catakism (Talking About Cats)

Of course, every Catakist loves to talk *about* their kitties, past and present. No topic of conversation, from hot sex gossip to politics to the meaning of life, is as fascinating as talking about one's own kitty.

Here are the three main topics of conversation around which the gospel of Catakism revolves:

My cat is so cute. How do you get a Catakist to talk about how cute her cat is? Answer: Remove the gag from her mouth. Anytime a believer is not conducting some other vital bit of cat business that actively engages her mouth—such as praising her cat or kissing her cat—she is, by default, talking about how cute her cat is. The real question is how do you *stop* a Catakist from talking about how cute her cat is? You can't.

My cat is so smart. Every Catakist is convinced that his kitty is Stephen Pawking, Isaac Mewton, Garry Catsparov, and Alpurrt Einstein all rolled into one and looks for any opportunity to talk about how smart kitty is. Want to start a "my cat is so smart" conversation with a believer? No, of course you don't. But you're going to do it anyway just by accidentally blurting out the word "intelligent" or "brain." The Catakist lies in wait for such a verbal trigger and then pounces like, well, a cat in the grass.

Example:

Normal person: "So we went to the parent-teacher conference, and Mrs. Perkins said that, based on Amy's IQ . . ."

Catakist: "My cat's IQ is so high, he can open doors with his paws."

Normal person (cont'd) ". . . she should be able to handle the assignments. It's not a question of her intelligence . . ."

Catakist: "My cat's so intelligent, he can tell time."

Normal person (cont'd) ". . . it's more a question of us creating the right learning environment for her at home. We need to make sure her room is nice and bright . . ."

Catakist: "My cat is so bright, he knows the word "fish" in fifteen languages.

Normal person (cont'd) ". . . that all her pencils and crayons are sharp . . ."

Catakist: "My cat's so sharp, he turns tampons into nesting material to trap mice."

Normal person (cont'd) "Are you listening to a word I say? God, if I had half a brain . . ."

Catakist: "My cat's so brainy, he designed and built his newest cat post"

Normal person (cont'd) "Never mind.

My cat is so weird. One of the main reasons Catakism exists on Earth is that cats never stop surprising humans. Just when you think you're coming close to figuring out what makes cats tick, another cat comes along with another mystifying behavior that is totally incomprehensible. Every cat walking the planet has at least one baffling quirk.

Here are just a few quirky habits Catakists have shared:

- the cat who steals thumbtacks from a corkboard and places them in her human's shoes
- the cat who licks the human's hair dryer for ten minutes every day
- the cat who deposits potatoes into the human's bed at night
- the cat who loves the show *Pretty Little Liars*, but nothing else on TV
- the cat who freaks out anytime the French national anthem plays

When it comes to "my cat is so weird" tales, humans never run out of material.

THE BOOK OF HAIR BALLS

The Rituals of Catakism

I. The Great Mystery

Is it a regurgitated mouse?

Is it a disembodied animal paw?

Is it an alien life form that just crawled off a meteorite?

Is it a dog turd wearing a cashmere sweater?

Is it a wet Tootsie Roll that was dropped on a barbershop floor?

Is it a sea cucumber turned inside out?

Is it the contents from a petri dish from the Plague Research Lab?

No, it's far worse. It's a hair ball!

No feline ritual causes more shock and horror among humans than the hawking up of the hair ball. Why is it, wonders the human, that a being as exalted as Cat—a being that keeps itself cleaner than surgical equipment, that sleeps only on silk pillows, that doesn't like to be watched when urinating—thinks nothing of hacking up a giant glob of fur held together with phlegm in the middle of the coffee table while the future in-laws are over for dinner?

The hawking up of the hair ball exemplifies the enigma that is Cat and humanity's utter inability to wrap its collective head around it.

The hawking up of the hair ball stands as a symbol for the vast array of incredible gross-outs, inconveniences, and drawbacks humans willingly put up with in order to be granted the sacred honor of playing lifelong servant to Cat. Let's face it—and even die-hard Catakists must admit this—cats bring a lot of, um, baggage with them. In fact, if you objectively listed all the dubious *perks* that come with living with a cat, one would think you were in the midst of a brainstorming session for Stephen King's next novel.

Just to mention a few:

Claws—Next to diamond-blade surgical scalpels, cat claws are the sharpest objects on Earth. A cat's paw is basically a cactus with retractable thorns. When cats aren't methodically jabbing their claws into our thighs, faces, bellies, and genitalia, they are raking them across our eighteenth-century furniture, reducing it to high-grade kindling. True Catakists willingly submit to this torture.

Dander—Dander is the dried-up remnants of cat skin that scatters itself across our homes like winter's first snow and nestles in sofa cushions, heating vents, and mattresses. About 30 percent of humans are seriously allergic to cat dander, but the idea that something as trivial as asthma, wheezing, coughing, sneezing, itchy eyes, rashes, hives, facial pain, shortness of breath, and tightness in the chest would be enough to make any card-carrying member of the Catakism faith consider *not* getting a cat is as absurd as the notion that cats *can't* teleport into closed spaces.

Cat pee—Second only to skunk spray on the list of the least congenial-smelling secretions in the animal kingdom. This wouldn't be so bad if cats limited their urinary expressions to the litter box, but cats have the ability to spray urine *onto vertical surfaces*, like your treasured Louis XV Bergère chair. Though the average obsessed cat lover spends more money on Febreze than on mortgage payments, she eventually learns that the odor of cat urine cannot be masked by any means.

Fleas—Though most cat people (and *all* cats) would insist, "My Snowball doesn't have fleas," the fact that the most widespread species of flea on Earth is the cat flea (*Ctenocephalides felis*) suggests otherwise. When your cat scratches itself hard enough to rattle your bowling ball off the shelf, it is not exfoliating; it is ex*termin*ating.

Vocalizations—Remember that silent Siamese beauty who charmed you into writing a four-figure check to *Couture de Chat*? Well, the minute you got her home, she began to demonstrate her startling vocal range . . . and she hasn't stopped making noise since. Cats, especially Siamese cats and cats seeking nonplatonic relationships, emit a collection of sounds custom-designed to penetrate the human cranium and muddle its contents. These noises—imagine a weed whacker in a tuba or a warthog being waterboarded—render all human thought impossible.

Kitty "friends"—Thanks to the aforementioned noises, which the cat broadcasts from every window in the house, cats attract a never-ending stream of feline guests to the human home. These consist of romantic suitors, cat enemies whose territory has been invaded and are ready to conduct *Gladiator*-style battles in the backyard, and kitties who are checking out your home and deciding whether or not they'd like to move in. When a human gets a cat, a human gets cats.

Vomit, hair balls, and assorted piles of moist matter—Kitties have an insistent habit of taking what's *inside* their bodies and placing it *outside* their bodies for humans to step in unaware. While in most cases they can be identified as vomit, poop, or hair balls, some feline "deliveries" defy explanation or categorization. Scoop it up, dispatch of it quickly, and pretend it never happened.

Homicidal thoughts—Nearly all Catakists, if they're being honest, occasionally harbor the belief that their cat is out to kill them. Maybe it's that cold glare in Tiddlywinks's eyes when you try to clip her nails or move her dish. Or maybe it's just that deep down we know Cat is our master and we remain alive only by staying in her good graces. Whatever the reason, we all secretly suspect that ol' Tiddly sometimes calculatingly plots our demise. We may laugh about it and make jokes, but that's what we fear, isn't it?

Of course, the Catakist cheerfully puts up with these drawbacks and many more. Why? Because the idea of living without Cat is horrifying. To truly understand what a dedicated Catakist must go through in order to gleefully subjugate himself to a feline, one must examine the rituals of Catakism.

II. Catakism 101

Like any quality belief system, Catakism is supported by a great many rituals. Rituals are repeated, formalized behaviors that carry significance and meaning beyond the act itself. In the case of Catakism, two different species are involved, so there are two basic types of ritual: those practiced by cats, and those practiced by humans. These rituals are practiced with great dedication and regularity.

III. Cat Rituals Involving Humans

Cats engage in dozens of ceremonial rites on a daily basis, most of which are incomprehensible to humankind. In fact, incomprehensibility seems to be the very purpose of these rituals. Humans, you see, have an irksome tendency to think they understand the workings of the universe. And so cats, being the highly evolved creatures they are, bring the spiritual lesson of humility to Man by doing things that have no conceivable explanation in any universe. Here are just a few Cat rituals designed to keep Man intellectually humble.

The dissection of the small mammal on the human's sofa. Though cats know that humans are repulsed by the sight of animal innards, a cat will insist on dismembering Minnie on the very seat cushion where the human's buttocks typically reside, then stare at the human with proud, innocent eyes that say, "Look what I did for you." This puts the human in the horrible position of either thanking the cat for the gift, which will only encourage more gifts of the same kind, or acting ungrateful, which is an eternal sin against cat. The human's head duly explodes.

The spontaneous clearing of the bookshelf. Every so often a cat will suddenly decide that its human has gotten all of the knowledge possible out of his/her self-help book collection and will clear an entire bookshelf, knocking its contents to the floor. Bookshelf-clearing typically takes place between the hours of one and four in the morning, usually on the night before a major presentation at work.

The biting of the hand that feeds. When word went out in the animal kingdom that it was not a particularly good idea to mangle the flesh of the being that provides your daily nourishment, evidently Cat was napping and didn't get the memo. Every now and then, a cat will engage in the spontaneous act of biting the literal hand that feeds her, viciously and without reason or provocation. Fortunately for the cat, the human will dismiss the behavior as a "love bite," as she is carted off to the ER for stitches and a tetanus shot. The human probably deserved it anyway, just ask the cat.

The need to stroll across the kitchen table right after using the litter box. Cats do appear to get extreme pleasure from walking on any surface that humans attempt to keep clean and germ-free. Chief among these are food-handling surfaces, such as counters, kitchen tables, and cutting boards. The probability of a cat walking on a food-handling surface is directly proportionate to the recency of the cat's litter box usage and the proximity of house guests you are trying to impress.

Ever wonder what those little kitty footprints on the counter are *made* of? Don't ask.

The random entropy lesson. Whenever a human attempts to complete a chore that involves gathering widespread particles into a concentrated pile—for example, sweeping a floor—a cat will come flying in from out of nowhere and redistribute the particles evenly throughout the room. Perhaps kitties do this because they want to teach humans lessons on the second law of thermodynamics, but there is the distinct possibility that they only do this to eff with us.

The giving of the piano recital at midnight. Though cats make a point of showing disdain for all human-created objects that make noise (except for the can opener), they insist on jumping on pianos and becoming Jerry Flea Lewis at 12:07 a.m.

The reconfiguration of the electronic device. Cats disapprove of the technological revolution that has turned humans into a race of zombies with their eyes glued to small electronic screens. (Eyes should be glued only to kitties.) They show their disapproval by pushing buttons and keys on our electronic devices and rendering them permanently nonfunctional. When the human pushes the Candy Crush icon on the iPad and the living room curtain starts opening and closing, there is only one explanation: Cat.

The galloping head-slam. Some kitties, for no apparent reason, give their humans more head-butts than a thug in a Guy Ritchie movie. These are not gentle head taps, but full cranial smashes preceded by a running gallop across a table. When the kitty skull collides with the human's, the force is enough to loosen dental work and cause concussions, but still the human insists the kitty is trying to show love to the human.

The presentation of the royal butt. There has long been discussion in cat circles as to why a cat will climb onto the lap of a human it likes, lift its tail, and present its feline . . . um, er, ah, *loaf pincher*, in all its sphincteric glory, to the unsuspecting human. The reason for this ritual is actually extremely obvious. The cat is just saying, "You're going to be kissing my a** for the rest of my life anyway, might as well get started now."

One of the reasons we revere cats so highly is that, try as we might, we can never figure them out. Thus, we can never feel intellectually superior to them. They are constantly testing us, performing rituals that are just beyond our comprehension.

IV. Human Rituals Involving Cats

From morning till night, Catakists perform a series of cat-related rituals that not only fail to benefit the cat toward which the rituals are aimed, but also fail to benefit themselves. Catakism rituals serve no practical purpose whatsoever; therefore, one must conclude that they are purely ceremonial in nature. Humans employ them for spiritual reasons—in order to keep themselves mindful of their cats and of the blissfully subservient position humans hold in relation to them.

The pointless calling of the kitty. Numerous times throughout the day, the Catakist, not having seen or praised Cat for an entire three and a half minutes, will call out its name repeatedly. In response, the cat dutifully does absolutely nothing. Unlike Dog. The only time cats come when called is mealtime, for which they were planning to come anyway.

The mystical opening/closing of the door (or window). Humans have a simple relationship with doors. When they want to enter or exit a room, they open a door, step through it, and close it again. Done. The mistake they make is to assume that cats have a similar relationship with doors. So when they see a kitty sitting expectantly near a door, they open it, figuring the kitty will simply pass through so the door may be shut again. Foolish human.

An open door is an opportunity for kitty to mess with a human. Kitty might decide to sit there without moving, dash out the doorway and right back in again, stand in the middle of the doorway, or go through the doorway, wait for the human to shut the door, then cry endlessly from the other side of the closed door until the human opens it again . . . as is his sworn duty to Cat.

The fruitless attempt to work in the presence of Cat. One of the most adorable human rituals is their ~~dogged~~ *catted* insistence on trying to get a job done when a cat has arrived on the scene. Cats are on a "mission from God" to disrupt all human activity that does not directly serve kitties. And yet humans valiantly attempt to do things like: fill out paperwork, write a book, chop vegetables, build a model, or paint a room, and cat is determined to "help." It would be easier for the human to play Jenga on a sailboat during a windstorm than accomplish their task with kitty's help.

The transfer of the sleeping cat from the lap to a new location. Occasionally, a human will get the deluded idea that what *he* needs to do—e.g., go to work, host the Oscars, deliver an inaugural address—is more important than a cat's nap and will make an attempt to move a sleeping kitty from his lap to a new location. With the delicate precision of an explosives specialist trying to defuse a bomb, he will slide his hands under the sleeping cat, lift up its curled form, and carry it across the room to a new (soft and warm) location.

The cat will remain asleep until the last moment, lulling the human into thinking he has achieved what no man hath done before. But then, just as the human is setting kitty down, the kitty will awaken, let out a "myawp," and scurry out of the room, giving the human the Glare of Damnation over its shoulder.

Ninefold Path Guidepost #7

It is never permissible to move a sleeping cat.

Every human since the beginning of time—certainly every Catakist—has known that it is against the laws of God, man, and nature to move a sleeping cat. Thus, when a cat goes to sleep on a human lap, that human is entrusted with the sacred duty of remaining locked in that bodily position until the cat finally decides to move. This can take any-where from one to five hours.

Not only is it sinful to remove a sleeping cat from a lap, but it is also grievously sinful to remove a sleeping cat from:

- ❧ *A coat or jacket*—Looks like you're staying for another drink after all.
- ❧ *"Important" papers*—How important can they be compared to a cat?
- ❧ *A mouse pad or keyboard*—Thinking of getting some work done? Think again.
- ❧ *Kitchen table*—I have an idea; let's eat on the floor tonight.
- ❧ *A human's bed*—We can sleep *around* Bootsy, right?

If you do wake a sleeping kitty, don't bother trying to make it up to her. The damage is done; you are now going to spend eternity in a very warm place. The good news is, according to a popular cat show on Animal Planet, there are cats there too!

The opening of the cat food can to lure a cat into a carrier. The instant a human picks up a cat carrier—correction: the instant a human *thinks* about picking up a cat carrier—all cats in the household dematerialize. The human then thinks: *Maybe if I open a can of cat food, I can lure the kitty out of hiding and trick it into the carrier for a nice trip to the vet.* The human proceeds with this seemingly logical plan and opens a can. The cat struts into the room, heads for the food dish expecting the human to serve her, but then spies the carrier and runs off before said human can capture her and lock her up for all eternity. Now the cat thinks: *The game has begun!* The human, buoyed by his near success, opens another can of cat food in order to create the luring sound again. This time, the cat shows up cautiously in the doorway and just as quickly disappears. At this point, the human moans, "What am I going to do with these open cans of cat food?" Ms. Bella knows.

The uttering of polite phrases to a cat. Catakists so thoroughly accept their cats as superior beings that they routinely display better social manners to their kitty than they do to fellow humans. Thus, they find themselves saying, "excuse me," when they need to walk past a cat and "sorry" if they accidentally jostle her. All requests made of the kitty (a Catakist never *commands* a cat; that's for the dogs) are preceded by "please" and followed by "thank you." And every (adorable) kitty sneeze merits a "God bless you." Some Catakists have even been heard to say, while offering the cat a selection of canned seafood pâtés to choose from, "An excellent choice, madam, and might I recommend a nice Riesling to go with that?"

The temporary erecting of the Christmas tree. Every year at Christmastime, a large percentage of Catakists place a giant cat toy in the middle of their living room, which they call a Christmas tree. Its branches bedecked with colorful balls, dangling doodads, and flashing lights, it is the most perfect kitty magnet known to man. Why then are new Catakists surprised when they awaken one morning to find the tree has been toppled over, while creating yet another Christmastime staple, the yule log? Any Catakist who has celebrated the season before knows that if the tree's not sufficiently "locked down," then it will be knocked over. One cannot possibly leave Precious home alone while the candles in the menorah are burning!

The deconstruction of the cat name. For Catakists, the process of choosing a name for a cat is undertaken with more seriousness of purpose than choosing a mate, a home, a college, or a career. However, the *instant* the name is given to the cat, the Catakist starts calling the cat something else. Tiberius, for example, immediately becomes Mr. Tibs. Then TT. Then TT the Squeegee. Then Mr. Squeege. Then Neezums, Squeezy-Neezie, Squishy-Squeezy, Mr. Squish, and before you know it, Tiberius is now Señor Squiddles.

In a Catakist home, a cat is rarely called the same name more than twice, after which the name devolves into another *cute* variation. Which *may*—just a possibility here—help explain why cats don't come when they're called.

The cat purr-formance art. Every Catakist has performed with Cat as the only audience, and many do so on a daily basis. This purr-formance art can range from the simple substitution of the cat's name in a song lyric to full song-and-dance numbers, accompanied by piano, and written and choreographed with kitty in mind. Kitty's reactions to this purr-formance art range from fear to indifference to bewilderment to plaintive yowling. Never ever does anything approaching enjoyment register on the cat's face.

The photographing of the cat doing, well, anything. Every Catakist has a deep and abiding belief in the supreme adorability of his own kitty, and so he wears out cell phone after cell phone taking photos of his cat doing remarkable things like eating, sitting, sleeping, stretching, and licking himself. The Cloud currently contains so many cat photos that one day soon it will literally begin raining cats.

V. Human Rituals That Don't Directly Involve the Cat

Finally, there are many rituals of Catakism that are performed without direct involvement of a live kitty. These are the cat-themed activities with which a Catakist fills his *spare time*; that is time not otherwise occupied by cuddling, praising, feeding, and talking to his cat. Such as:

The *sharing* of the photos of the cat doing anything. After taking his daily quota of the cat doing, literally, anything, the Catakist emails them to everyone on his contacts list and posts them on multiple social media sites with captions such as, "Oops, you caught me," and "Sleepin' it off."

The making of the Christmas Card in which the cat is prominently featured. Make that, the cat is the only family member pictured on the card. For a photo of this magnitude, the kitty needs to be posed with a *real* Santa, and it needs to be taken by a professional photographer, specifically one with at least ten years of pet portraiture experience.

The commenting on other Catakists' photos of their fur babies. There is a quid pro quo in Catakism: I will write adoring comments about your cat's photos if you do the same for mine. So whenever a Catakism practitioner is not admiring photos of her own kitty, she is admiring and commenting on photos of friends' cats while secretly opining that they are not quite as adorable as her own. "Friendships" on Facebook and followings on Twitter are terminated daily due to the nonreciprocal praise of one's cat.

Other rituals include:

- the baking of cat-themed cakes and cookies
- the making of cat-themed crafts
- the teaching of the toddler how to draw cats
- the shopping for cat-themed clothes
- the buying of cat knickknacks
- the decorating of the house in feline themes
- the watching of cat programs and videos
- et catera, et catera, et catera

Every Catakist knows this basic bit of catma. Any time spent *not* doing cat-related rituals is time wasted. The only way to do penance for this is to double or triple up on cat rituals at the next opportunity—for instance, watching a cat show on TV *while* knitting a cat sweater, drinking tea out of a cat mug, and cuddling with a cat.

THE BOOK OF THE MOUSE

The mysterious connection between cats and computers

I. Cat and Mouse

Cats and mice are the classic predator and prey. Throughout history, it was the small, furry—and apparently delicious—mammal that captivated Cat's attention, but nowadays cats have also developed a mystical connection to the *electronic* mouse that sits on our desks.

Cats and computers have joined forces in a mysterious way that no one could have predicted thirty years ago. There's nothing inherently feline about a metal box containing a motherboard, CPU, and graphics card, yet wherever computers are found, we also find cat obsession. The Internet and social media, in fact, have become the primary place of worship for Catakists the world over, with thousands of websites devoted to kitties and endless tidal waves of cat videos and memes clogging up the cyber highways. Yes, computers, tablets, and smartphones have become the new vehicle for sharing the essential catechism of Catakism.

The computer phenomenon cuts both ways. Cats are fascinated by computers, and computer users are fascinated by cats. This connection between computer users and cats has never been scientifically explored—until now. But one thing is for sure: the more a human uses a computer to make a living or fill spare time, the more likely that human is to have an emotional attachment to cats.

Whereas dog owners tend to be active, outdoorsy types who drive Jeeps, hang out at the beach, and play Frisbee, cat owners tend to write software, knit, and download cooking apps. Of course, this isn't a hard-and-fast rule—Catakists come in all sizes and preferences—but in general, the more chair-bound and computer-centric a human's lifestyle, the more likely kitties play a major role in his or her life.

Turns out, there is an underlying historical reason for this . . . read on.

II. In the Beginning: a Small Rodent
In order to understand how computers and cats became connected, one must go way back to the very origins of Man's relationship with Cat.

It all began with the mouse, the small rodent with the pointed snout, large ears, and a tendency to reproduce faster than fruit flies. Cats first caught the eye of Man when felines started staking out grain houses and devouring the mice that devoured the grains. This was a win/win arrangement for humans and cats—for mice, not so much. But the most important thing to note about this symbiotic relationship is the *type* of human with whom cats formed their early partnership. The humans who had large stores of nuts, grains, and berries were, of course, *gatherers*.

Whereas dogs have always been closely aligned with the *hunter* strain of Man, cats have always been closely aligned with the *gatherer* strain.

III. Behold the Mighty Gatherer

The term *hunter-gatherer* is often hyphenated, as if hunting and gathering were closely related activities, but nothing could be further from the truth. Hunters and gatherers have always been very different types of creatures and have developed into two distinct lineages throughout human history.

Hunters were aggressive and athletic. They loved the thrill of the chase and the excitement of the kill. And because refrigeration was not a gleam in mankind's eye until the eighteenth century, meat could be stored and had to be eaten fresh. That meant hunters had to hunt every day, which kept them active and in great shape.

When hunters ate the flesh of their prey, they also ingested its adrenaline, making them even more aggressive and warlike. Hunters evolved into the active and assertive personalities of today—soldiers, hockey players, currency traders. Hunters have always had a close relationship with dogs, who love to run, hunt, wrestle, eat red meat, and fight alongside their human partners.

Gatherers had a slightly different orientation. They sought the thrill of the well-dropped piece of fruit, the excitement of the slowly ripening berry, the suspense of the nicely yeasted bread dough (would it rise to make a perfect loaf, or sink?). Their nuts and grains could be stored for weeks, even months or years, so if they didn't go out and gather today, well, there was always tomorrow.

Gatherers learned how to kick back and stay warm during the long winter months when there was nothing to gather. Gatherers evolved into farmers, who evolved into landowners, who evolved into scholars, who evolved into scientists and engineers, who evolved into software developers and computer junkies.

Note the pronounced lack of running, jumping, and climbing required.

Gatherers have always had a close relationship with cats, who love to nap, watch stuff happen *outside* the window, and stay in the house, where it's nice and dry.

The Hunter-Gatherer Test

Hunters and gatherers still exist today, but in modern form. Looking at the following two lists and see if you can guess which list represents the hunter strain and which represents the gatherer strain in today's world.

LIST A	LIST B
State policeman	Video game designer
NASCAR driver	Book editor
Fireman	Theoretical physicist
NFL linebacker	Hairstylist
Homicide detective	Video game tester
Drill sergeant	Call center support person
Helicopter pilot	English professor
EMT	Playwright
Bounty hunter	Video game reviewer
Sharpshooter	Flautist
Biker	Webmaster
Cowboy	Pastry chef
UFC fighter	Video gamer

Which list would be more likely to host cats in their homes? Sorry, no hints.

The Cat-Gatherer Connection

Until a few decades ago, hunters were the dominant strain of human on Earth, and therefore dogs were the most prominent pets. However, since the dawn of the Internet, when humans were no longer required to vacate their chairs in order to earn a living, gatherers have become the dominant strain. Could this be why cats are now more popular than dogs worldwide? The geekier we get as a culture, the more cats we invite into our lives.

IV. The Internet as Cat Park

Dog owners (i.e., the hunters of today) like to meet and hang with other dogs and dog owners. They do this in places called dog parks.

But, alas, there are no cat parks. Why not? After all, isn't the most elevated being on Earth worthy of its own gathering place? Well, not only would a cat park require kitties to do things like play nicely with others and stay where you put them, but it would also require cat *people* to do things like be outdoors.

So, no. No cat parks.

And because cat parks don't exist (except in Jackson Galaxy's fever dreams), cat people are forced to share their cat obsession online. *The Internet has become the dog park for cat owners.* It is the modern gathering place for talking about cats, looking at cats, reading about cats, *awww*ing about cats, bragging about cats, et *cat*era.

V. What Happens in the Cat Park Doesn't Stay in the Cat Park

The idea that the Internet is planet Earth's cat park is not just an amusing observation. It's a fact. According to Google, people search the term "cats" more than thirty million times a month. There was a recent exhibit at New York's Museum of the Moving Image called, "How Cats Took Over the Internet," and there's a popular book on Amazon that tells you how to make your cat an Internet celebrity. The Internet, once synonymous with porn, has now become synonymous with kitties (*oh stop it, the feline kind!*). In fact, the Internet has become so saturated with cats that it now spills over into our daily lives, even off the computer.

In recent years, cat lovers have been observed singing the "hit" Internet song "The Internet Is Made of Cats" around the office, wearing Grumpy Cat T-shirts, drinking from Lil Bub coffee mugs, reading *I Can Has Cheezburger?* books, and attending the world's first CatCon in Los Angeles, where more than ten thousand visitors paid tribute to Internet-famous cats in 2016.

Internet cat love transcends national borders and even offers a new model of how humanity can get along peacefully. Whereas virtually every other online topic invites commentary like, "Nice idea, moron," cat lovers by the hundreds of millions communicate respectfully and supportively with one another online.

So what actually goes on in this magical, peace-loving global cat park that is the Internet? As if you didn't know!

VI. The Watching and the Sharing of Cat Videos

There was a time when baseball was considered America's favorite pastime. Obviously, this was before computers. Now, watching cat videos has become America's—nay, the *world's*—favorite pastime.

Cat YouTube videos offer clear proof of the Cat-a-gorical Imperative, which calls for the simultaneous regarding of cats as dignified and worship-worthy, cute and cuddly, and ridiculously funny. To a Catakist, there is no contradiction amongst these three mandates. And cat You-Tube videos cover all three bases.

1. **Dignified and worship-worthy.** These videos capture cats doing things like outsmarting dogs, maintaining their dignity in absurd

situations, and "disciplining" humans and other creatures with swatting paws and stern expressions. Others show cats eating, drinking, and pooping in dignified and proper ways. Catakists like to be reminded that cats are above all other beings.

2. **Cute and cuddly.** Catakists love to revel in the infinite cuteness of cats, so there are millions of Internet videos of cats cuddling with puppies, playing with ducklings, sleeping in cute ways, and staring at you with gigantic eyes. If you listen carefully about thirty seconds after the posting of a new kitty video on YouTube, you'll hear a collective "awww" rising up across the globe.

3. **Ridiculously funny.** Most of all, Catakists like to laugh themselves sick over cats. On the surface, this seems like odd behavior for humans who spend their lives placing cats on pedestals. On closer examination, though, it's a way of making the superior being seem more accessible to the masses, of bringing the great and powerful down to human level. And nothing accomplishes this more so than cats . . .

- trying to cram themselves into tiny boxes
- with objects stuck on their heads
- dressed in ridiculous costumes
- sleeping in goofy positions
- falling off high things
- being surprised by animals and gadgets
- interacting comically with mirrors
- sliding on slippery surfaces
- trying to figure out toilet paper rolls (obviously, over is preferred to under for optimal ease in unwinding)

If not for the guilty pleasure of watching cats being humiliated, Catakists might feel oppressed and subjugated by cats, and Catakism might feel like a burden. A daily dose of laughing at cats allows the human to preserve the illusion that humans are equal, and even superior (ha!), to cats and keeps the practice of Catakism light and enjoyable.

VII. The Paying of Tribute to Famous Cats

Before the invention of the Internet, it was not really possible for any individual kitty to become famous outside her local circle of admirers. But all that has changed, and every so often a special kitty will rise up from the ranks of the merely adored to become an object of true mass worship, attracting millions of followers. Internet-famous cats now garner more international recognition than world leaders, TV stars, and Kardashian body parts. Because of this new phenomenon, Catakists, in addition to worshipping *their own* kitties every day, must take time out of their busy lives to pay tribute to their favorite Internet cat(s).

What remarkable feats and talents have these famous cats exhibited in order to win the devotion of millions of worldwide admirers?

Cat	Talent/Claim to Fame	Career Success
Grumpy Cat	Misshapen muzzle makes her appear permanently displeased	TV appearances, Lifetime movie deal, Gund plush toy, bestselling books
Maru	Places self in containers too tight for body	Over 300 million video viewings, book, DVD
Lil BUB	Has tongue that is exposed at all times	Online merchandising empire including toys, calendars, cups, magnets, and bobbleheads
Hamilton the Hipster Cat	Muzzle resembles a white mustache	Instagram sensation, TV appearances
Colonel Meow (deceased, sniff)	Possessed long hair and perpetually "angry" expression.	350,000 Facebook followers, *Guiness Book of World Records* entry
Street Cat Bob	Hung out with a homeless guy	*New York Times* bestselling book, major movie deal
Nala	Has crossed eyes and short legs	2.5 million Facebook followers, merchandising empire

After studying the amazing accomplishments of these world-famous felines, it's easy to see why they have achieved the global recognition they have. Still, there is hope for kitties with less prodigious talents to also make their mark on the world stage, thanks to the global cat park known as the Internet.

Just make sure kitty has a good agent.

VIII. Cat Blogs: And Now, a Reading from Scripture

Every Catakist has a list of cat-themed blogs that are required daily online reading. In Catakism, these can be thought of as *sacred* readings, a way for believers to reaffirm their faith, learn new things about cats, and discover new ways to obsess over felines on a daily basis.

Cat blogs dispense wisdom, information, and advice on useful and practical topics such as:

- How to Keep Cats Calm During Fireworks
- Taking Better Cat Selfies
- Rating the Top Five Automated Mouse Toys
- Why Cats Love Cardboard Boxes
- Best Mobile Apps for Checking the Safety of Cat Food
- The Cat Food Wars: Dry vs. Wet
- Why Cats Like to Watch Us Pee

And, of course, there are the endless blogs written in the "voice" of cats, describing the world from a feline point of view. These blogs allow humans to imagine that they are really considering the world from a cat's perspective, when, in fact, they are considering things from the perspective of a human *imagining* what a cat wants to say. When a cat *really* has something she needs to tell you, she'll vomit on your pillow and make sure you know.

IX. The Sharing of Cat Stories

The Internet is also the number one outlet for sharing cat stories. Cat stories are most effective when they begin with a tragic circumstance and end with a heartwarming resolution, leaving not a dry eye on the Web. Thus, most cat stories fall into one of the following cat-a-gories:

- Cat becomes reunited with former *owner* after long separation, changing everyone's lives for the better.
- Human at low point in life adopts rescue cat, changing everyone's lives for the better.
- Cat with missing limbs or other physical challenges learns to live fully, changing everyone's lives for the better.

- Cat "adopts" animal of another species, changing everyone's lives for the better.
- Cat saves life of human with medical condition, changing everyone's lives for the better.

An immutable principle of Catakism is that every Catakist has numerous stories about his or her cat(s) that they think are worthy of being made into books, TV shows, and movies—Pixar might beg to differ.

X. Feline Productivity Enhancers

In addition to all the wonderfully entertaining and leisurely uses of the Internet listed above, there are also times during the course of each day where a Catakist just needs to buckle down and get some serious work done. Fortunately, there's an infinite number of cat-themed websites out there dedicated to enhancing human productivity.

Just a few examples of some real cat websites that will surely help you through your workday:

- **Cat Bounce.** Features cats bouncing. Up and down. But wait, there's more—an interactive component! Drag each cat to a new position, *then* watch it bounce.
- **Dress a Cat.** Take a cat, dress it up. Done.
- **The Cat Scan.** Photos of cats on scanners, with their legs tucked under them. Amazing! Upload your own!
- **Meowmania.** Click a spot, a cat's head appears there. Yup, that's it.
- **The Infinite Cat Project.** Cats watching cats. In mirrors and monitors. To infinity.
- **Garfield Minus Garfield.** Garfield comic strips with Garfield Photoshopped out, leaving Jon Arbuckle talking to empty space.

- **Meowbify.** Takes any website, adds cat pictures and videos to it, and turns it into a cat site.
- **Procatinator.** Name says it all. Short, animated cat GIFs paired with songs that match the GIF's rhythm.
- **The Kitten Covers.** Famous album covers with, you guessed it, kittens replacing the orginal image.
- **My Cat Is an A**hole!** One of many cat-shaming sites (shame!). Submit photos of your cat acting like an a**hole.
- **Nyan Cat.** Observe a primitive animation of a cat with a pink Pop-Tart for a body running along, followed by a rainbow. Just because.

XI. Cat Computer "Help"

As obsessed as human computer users are with cats, cats are equally obsessed with computers. More accurately, they are obsessed with helping humans use their computers less effectively. Although DICKs may get angry when a cat interferes with their computer usage, Catakists welcome this *help* and view it as a sacred blessing, even as it costs them time, money, business, efficiency, and relationships.

Some typical forms of cat computer help include:

Stationing body in front of the monitor. At least once a day, the cat will slowly walk across the human's desk and sit in front of the monitor with a placid here-is-the-place-where-I-most-belong-on-Earth expression on her face. For the next hour or two, the human must crane his neck in all directions, trying to see *around* the cat, who remains stubbornly nontransparent.

Helping factor: The human gets some much-needed stretching, relieving neck tension.

Kneading the keyboard. At a critically important moment in the human's workday—e.g., solving the formula for cold fusion or replying to a Facebook friend request—the cat will stroll onto the keyboard, begin kneading it, and turn the human's work into character salad while Cat purrs contentedly.

Helping factor: Human gets a critical reminder about the importance of saving his work every ten seconds.

Batting the touch screen. Whenever the human is intensely engaged in a game or work activity on a tablet or smartphone, the cat's paw will dart in from the sidelines, batting at the screen as if it were a cat toy, and crashing whatever application the human was using. Eureka, touch screens work with paws too!

Helping factor: Human receives some free bug-testing of his software.

Sleeping on the mouse arm. For a large portion of the human's workday or World of Warcraft session (these activities may be done simultaneously), the cat will sleep with her body draped across the arm the human uses to operate the computer mouse or game controller. The Catakist will passively adapt to the added weight and carry on with his activity. Many video games now allow players to select this as an official difficulty level, so now they can choose from: Easy, Hard, Expert, or Cat Sleeping on Arm.

Helping factor: Human is forced to become ambidextrous.

Editing the email. Often when a human is in the middle of composing an email, she will get up to use the bathroom or get a drink only to return to her desk to find that her email has been "edited" by kitty. The true Catakist does not change the cat's literary contribution, but simply includes a parenthetical remark stating, respectfully, "(my cat's edits)."

Helping factor: Email recipient gets many bonus jjjjjjjjjjjjjjjjjjjjjjjjjjjjjjjjs in her email.

XII. The Cat and the App

The dedicated Catakist eventually decides it's time to get kitty her own apps to play with. Incredibly, these products actually exist. Yes, numerous cat apps are available for tablets and smartphones, including:

Chase the . . . mouse, frog, bug, ball, fish, laser dot. The majority of cat apps fall into the category of "thing moves around the screen, cat whacks it." The human, as usual, finds these games more amusing than the cat does. If it's a very realistic game, like some of the fishing apps, the cat will remain interested for a while until it figures out that it can't win the game, at which point it reverts to a game it *can* win: Make the Human Stroke the Cat for Three Straight Hours. The only real winner of cat games is Apple Inc., because after an hour of whacking and scratching by a cat, your iPad will need a new screen.

Human vs. Kitty game. This app pits a human player against a cat. The human flings things at a goal, the kitty tends the goal. In this case, it is the human who becomes bored when he quickly realizes that the cat is better at the game than he is. He then quietly deletes the app and mentions it to no one.

Human-to-Cat Translator. While this one is technically for cat *people* rather than cats, it *does* involve cats directly. The app purports to analyze the human's voice and "translate" it into cat sounds. Needless to say, it works about as well as a speed limit sign on a stretch of open road. The day all Catakists fear is the day the first *Cat-to-Human* Translator app is released. For then humans may hear that kitty is actually saying, "Come near me with that fake fish again and you're going to need a tetanus booster."

Ninefold Path Guidepost #8

The use of any image except your cat's as your social media profile pic is forbidden by sacred law

Got a nice photo of a spouse or fiancé you'd like to use online? Too bad.

Have children, nieces, or nephews you'd like to brag about? Sorry.
Is there a piece of artwork you enjoy looking at? Nuh-uh.
A recently deceased parent you wish to honor? No dice.
A special location you are in love with? Not gonna happen.
The only permissible image to use for your profile pic on ALL web-sites—as well as for the wallpaper on your smartphone, computer, and other electronic devices—is your cat's. Period. There are no exceptions to this rule.
Ye shalt be known forever online as the anonymous person behind the kitty.

THE BOOK OF LITTER

Kitty Litter, Litters of Kitties—Why Catakism Is Littered with Litter

I. Getting Litteral

Few words are more intimately connected to cats than the word "litter." The word, of course, has dual meaning in the world of cat stewardship: it's the stuff we fill litter boxes with, *and* it's the stuff cats fill our *homes* with—namely, litters of kittens. Think of the word *litter* and you think *cat* or *kitty*.

Both meanings of the word are central to Catakism, because they both represent two totally natural feline processes—elimination and reproduction—that cats are perfectly capable of handling on their own but that Catakists insist on "managing." Believers insert themselves into these processes because of their need to feel needed by cats. The thought that cats can get by perfectly well without them is too terrifying for the true believer to contemplate.

The way we handle both litter boxes and boxes of litters is emblematic of the entire Catakistic process.

What few people realize, many Catakists included, is that litter—that stuff that comes in industrial-size bags and for which there is no known legitimate way to dispose of once it has been soaked with, um, *liquid gold*—is almost single-handedly responsible for the rise of modern Catakism. It allowed cats and humans to develop the cozy domestic relationship they currently enjoy.

It's true. Without cat litter, there would be no pink nail pawlish, no cat videos, no crystal stemware filled with gourmet poached prawn. Essentially no Catakism. And there is an actual legitimate historic reason for this (no joke).

II. The "Saints" of Catakism

If Catakism had saints—of the human variety (it certainly has kitty saints, millions of them)—there are two figures who would stand at the very top of the holy panoply: Ed Lowe and Kay Draper. For it was a chance encounter between these two humans in 1947 that gave rise to the greatest single invention in the history of Catakism. Cat litter.

From a Catakist's perspective, the meeting of Lowe and Draper has the significance of Lennon meeting McCartney, of chocolate meeting peanut butter, of macaroni meeting cheese. Without these two humans, cat litter might never have been invented, and Catakism might still be wallowing in the dark ages.

To understand the significance of the movement these two seemingly unremarkable people launched, we need to travel back in time.

Cats Didn't Always Sleep on the Tem-purr-pedic!

From the time of Man's first meeting with Cat thousands of years ago until the end of World War II, cats and humans had a cordial, but *detached* relationship with each other. Humans lived in the nice, clean, warm homes, and cats lived outdoors. Cats would come around to visit, and humans would feed and stroke them, but kitties basically remained outdoor animals. Wild, free, self-sustaining. At best they lived in human garages and barns, where they played the role of "mouser."

By the time of the great World Wars, though, many humans, longing for a closer relationship with Jinx and Bobtail, had begun to put out old baking pans filled with sand, sawdust, ashes, or shredded paper for their cat friends to poop in, and cats had begun obliging. These pans, however, were placed in garages or back entryways, not in the heart of the human home.

And then it happened . . .

III. The "Kitty Hawk" Moment

Ed Lowe had a family business that sold industrial absorbents, such as sand, sawdust, and kiln-dried clay, which were used for soaking up oil spills around machinery. One day, Ed's neighbor, Kay Draper, came to his door and asked if he had any sand she could use for her cat box, because she was tired of cleaning up little pee-scented ash footprints. Ed's stock of sand was frozen solid, so he suggested she try the dried-clay product, which was called Fuller's Earth, instead. Ed then forgot about the whole thing.

Two weeks later, Kay came back to his door looking for more Fuller's Earth and raving that not only was it much more absorbent than sand or ash, but that it also controlled odor much better. The kitties loved it too. Lowe realized he was on to something. He re-bagged some of his product, wrote "kitty litter" on the bags, and brought them to the local hardware store to sell. He then began demonstrating his product at cat shows and crisscrossed the country, selling it at pet shops, hardware stores, and out of the trunk of his car.

And thus an empire was born. (And, in effect, so was Catakism.) In 1964, Lowe created the Tidy Cat company, and by the end of his life he dominated a half-billion-dollar-a-year industry. The PBS show *Small Business School* credits him for being the quintessential entrepreneur who built a "huge business from nothing"—though it could more accurately be said that he built a huge business from sh**.

IV. The Historical Significance

The birth of kitty litter was a monumental turning point in human-feline relations and represents the birth of modern Catakism. Why? Because it was at that precise moment that cats officially began pooping and peeing *inside* human homes. This immediately led to them *living* in human homes 24/7 and *giving birth* in human homes, and holding court over them three hundred and sixty-five days a year.

The birth of litter was the birth of the feline as a domestic creature fully under the care and feeding of humans. This was also the birth of the human as a submissive creature fully under the control and mastery of cats. Litter was the brilliant invention that led to the origin of nearly all of the trappings of hardcore Catakism: the climate-controlled cat condos, the gourmet entrées, the Santa hats, the cat hotels, et *catera*.

So thank you Ed Lowe and Kay Draper. Without your invaluable contribution, cats might still be under the illusion that they could poop, pee, eat, drink, and have kittens outdoors, on their own. And where would that leave millions of dedicated Catakists? With way too much free time on their hands.

V. The Evolution of Litter

To appreciate the brave new world that Catakism has created since the invention of litter, one need only look at the evolution of litter itself. A few short decades ago it came in one variety: regular. Today there is a cornucopia of competing products that fills an entire aisle of the supermarket and leaves the novice cat worshiper as confused as the father of a teenage girl staring in horror at the wall of feminine hygiene products.

The variety of cat litter available is evidence of the absurd level of fanaticism we show toward cats. We have created this finely customized world for cats and cats only. Why? Not because cats need it, but because it makes *us* feel better to know we are serving our master at the highest level possible. It's all about us, right?

Here are just a few of the features and refinements that have been added to cat litter, and from which the dedicated Catakist must now carefully choose:

- ❧ **Odor-locking/odor-neutralizing crystals.** No one knows what these mysterious blue crystals are made of (though they look suspiciously like a famous blue crystal product manufactured by a guy known as Heisenberg), but consumers are urged to believe that they not only *cover up* odors, but lure them in and trap them in hermetically sealed crystalline chambers.
- ❧ **Advanced clumping.** Clumping is a highly desirable feature in cat litter because who doesn't want nice tight clumps of cat urine? *Regular* clumping? Please. Only *advanced* clumping for Catakists.
- ❧ **Sealing.** What exactly is "sealing" as it pertains to litter? No one knows for sure; perhaps an army of miniature SWAT technicians kipnaps your cat's feces and coats them in quick-sealing industrial enamel.
- ❧ **Bacteria control.** Because it's vital that litter's bacteria be tightly controlled.
- ❧ **Multi-cat formula.** No litter manufacturer has ever explained the actual difference between cat litter designed for one cat and cat litter designed for multiple cats. Does the multi-cat brand hand out monogrammed moist towels to each distinct user? Perhaps they should.
- ❧ **Scoopable.** It is important that kitty litter be "scoopable," because, as we all know, the bargain-brand variety is physically repelled by scoops, making it impossible to dig out of the box.
- ❧ **24/7 performance.** It is not entirely clear what "performance" a bed of absorbent granules is expected to put on, but clearly no one wants a litter that only performs twenty-three hours a

day, then takes a break to go hang out in the green room with the backup singers.

❖ **Dust-free.** Because who wants to scoop up dusty cat poop?

Cat fanatics are not put off by all these choices. Rather, they *love* to have such options to consider, so they can convince themselves they are doing a conscientious and thorough job of overly caring for their cats.

VI. Boxes or Biodomes?

As fast as cat litter technology has been evolving, litter *box* technology has been evolving even faster. Catakists regard kitties as such ascended beings that they are driven to convince both themselves and their cats that modern felines no longer have an actual biological need to poop. And so they buy increasingly elaborate and sterile-looking structures meant to disguise the process from human eyes (and noses). Today it is virtually impossible to tell a cat's litter box from a time travel machine, except for the fact that most people who own a time travel machine don't put it on the floor and let their cats crap in it.

There are litter box models that resemble salon hair dryers, copying machines, human toilets, and giant hamster wheels and cost up to $500. All have a futuristic design intended to be as far removed from crapping-on-the-forest-floor as possible. Have any of these new technologies succeeded in changing the basic way that poop comes out of a cat? Alas, no, poop still emerges from cats the old-fashioned way. But there are a myriad of technologies for dealing with the poop once it has landed so that humans can pretend cat poop doesn't exist and the cat can remain a perfectly spiritual being in the human's mind.

The most exciting of these technologies are the self-cleaning models. There are litter boxes that rake the litter and deposit the "results" into a bag for easy disposal. There are rotating-wheel designs that sift out the poop like mining equipment seeking gold. There are models with live plumbing that rinse the reusable plastic litter pellets with water and flush the waste away like a human toilet.

And there are also rumored to be some new designs in the works, patents pending:

The Crapatorium—Kitty poops on a conveyor belt, then the results are "cremated" in a tiny oven at 2300 degrees Fahrenheit. Ashes may be placed in decorative vials.

Pneumat-o-cat—Tinkerbell's turds are sucked up into a pneumatic suction tube, like the ones banks once use at drive-throughs, and are deposited in the neighbor's yard.

The Crap-a-pult—Low-tech, low-cost version of the above. It just *flings* the poop into the neighbor's pool.

The Tom-poster—Packages kitty's waste in tiny sterile bags labeled "Fertilizer." Congratulations, your cat doesn't poop, she gardens.

Schrodinger's Catbox—By flipping a quantum switch, you create an alternate universe in which the cat never pooped in the first place.

All litter box technology is designed for one end (no, not that one), and one end only: to make it easier for the common cat obssesser to pay homage to their kitties by denying that cats have the same appalling digestive processes we do.

VII. The Posterior Power Play
There is an even deeper psychological principle at work in humans' takeover of cats' excretory processes. That is, humans have voluntarily assumed a lower position on life's totem pole than cats. As Jerry Seinfeld once put it, "You see two life forms. One is making a poop, the other is carrying it for him. Who would you think is in charge?"

The powerful do not clean the toilets of the weak.

It is rumored that former president LBJ used to conduct informal cabinet meetings while perched on the toilet. By doing so, he placed himself in a higher power position than those around him. In effect, he was saying, "You have to deal with my pooping; I don't have to deal with yours."

This principle is known as the Posterior Power Play.

By delegating their poop management to humans, cats have pulled off the ultimate coup and cemented their superior position to humans.

And Catakists happily play along.

VIII. Litter Cakes: The Ultimate Symbol of Submission

If you have any doubts that humans take actual pleasure in humbling themselves to cats, google the term "kitty litter cake." The results may shock and appall you, or, if you're a diehard feline admirer, produce squeals of delight.

Yes, there is a popular confection, baked up in countless human homes, known at the litter cake. This is an edible dessert made from cake, crumbled cookies, and partially melted Tootsie Rolls and designed to look exactly like, yup, a used litter box. The confection is presented in a (hopefully new) plastic litter box and served with a (also preferably new) litter box sifting tool.

You might think this dessert was a one-time gag, dreamed up by someone with a twisted sense of humor and far too much time on his hands. But sadly, a Google search produces hundreds of photos of varying litter cake designs, as well as numerous competing recipes and discussion threads as to which recipe produces the best litter cake. Litter cake is a bona fide *thing*.

It doesn't take a Freudian analyst to grasp the psychological significance of this. By dining on the litter cake, we are symbolically eating, well, do we have to say it?

The point is: the kitty litter cake is the ultimate proof of the position humans have put themselves in relative to cats. In the Man vs. Cat power game, Cat has won and owns it.

Ninefold Path Guidepost #9

*When a cat emerges from a litter box,
pretend you weren't looking.*

Here is one area where cats and their people agree: cats don't poop. Got it? Good.

IX. The Other Litter: Kittens
Humans were so successful at taking over the excretory processes of cats that they have now taken over Cat's reproductive cycle as well.

Humans have become kitty midwives. Not because cats need us to be, but because, again, we need to be needed by cats.

The birth of kittens is an event of high religious significance in a Catakistic household. Therefore, it must be carefully overseen.

Only a few short decades ago, when a cat was ready to have kittens, she would seek out a private corner in the garage or barn, make herself a comfy nest, give birth to her litter, and nurse her kittens until they were ready to survive on their own. Period.

Humans now feel they must supervise every aspect of Cat's reproductive cycle, from which cat dude they get frisky with to when to buy booties for the kittens. They now do everything short of attending Lamaze classes with their cats. Judging by a human's behavior around kitty birth, an alien observer might conclude their motivation was: How can I interfere in this natural process so as to create maximum anxiety for myself, the cat, and the kittens?

X. Cat Birthing Steps for the Responsible Cat Owner

Veterinarians and cat experts now offer cat birth advice that goes miles beyond Dr. Benjamin Spock's famous book for humans. Some of the steps that actual cat care books and websites suggest are listed in bold; the Catakist's translation follows:

1. **Regularly monitor your cat for signs of pregnancy.** *Pin her down every forty-five minutes or so and give her an impromptu gynecological exam. That will surely drive her out the door, at which point she will likely return home pregnant. Yay, result attained. Salmon, pickles, and Häagen-Dazs for everyone!*

2. **If she appears pregnant, take her to a licensed veterinarian for a complete checkup.** *The vet will advise you as to the safety of the pregnancy, the estimated number of kittens to expect, and any pregnancy support groups in your area that you can attend.*

3. **Keep track of the pregnancy's duration.** *A cat going past sixty-seven days should receive an ultrasound and a possible caesarean section. (A cat going over eighty days is a cat hanging onto her pregnancy for dear life because she's terrified of the "help" you're going to offer at birth time.)*

4. **Change her diet in the third trimester.** *At forty-two days into the pregnancy, switch mom to kitten food. Of course the only way you will know she is forty-two days in is if you had a ringside seat to the conception. In which case, shame on you.*

5. **Set up a nest.** *Get a cardboard box with high sides, fill it with soft material, place it in a safe, warm place where mom will have easy access to food and a litter box . . . and then watch her proceed to ignore it and make a nest in your sock drawer instead.*

6. **Prepare your cat for kittens.** *Trim the hair around the birth area so the kittens have easy egress. Trim the hair around the nipples so the kittens have easy access.*

7. **Prepare for the birth.** *Have a cat carrier ready in case of an emergency trip to the vet. Keep your cell phone charged and your vet's number cued up. Have clean, dry towels ready for cleaning kittens. Have cat milk powder and a nursing bottle available in case the kittens don't nurse. Ask your doctor for a Valium prescription.*

8. **Watch for signs of medical issues.** *These can include a greenish-yellow, bright green, or reddish discharge; vomiting; diarrhea; sneezing; coughing; and loss of appetite—and that's just for you. The cat may have symptoms too.*

9. **Clean and sterilize your hands** *for at least five minutes with antimicrobial hand soap. After all, it is crucial to be absolutely sterile when assisting in a process that, until a few years ago, often took place in barns.*

10. **Watch for labor complications**, *such as listlessness, excessive grooming, restlessness, pacing, excessive purring, vomiting, a drop in body temperature below 102 degrees Fahrenheit, or loud crying. If you see any of these, increase your anxiety level. There's nothing else you can do.*

11. **Keep the environment calm.** *Which means, essentially, that YOU should leave the room. If you can't do that, at least stop repeating, "I hope I don't f*** up, I hope I don't f*** up," like a mantra.*
    And then things really kick into high gear . . .

12. **Monitor each delivery.** *Take some deep breaths.*

13. **Watch for contractions, which should be 2–3 minutes apart.** *Come on, breathe. You can do this.*

14. **Make sure mother breaks the amniotic sac.** *Have that phone handy to call 911. Where the &%$# is it?*

15. **Wipe the kitten's face with a clean, warm towel**. *More towels, more hot water!*

16. **Check that there is one placenta per kitten.** *Stay calm, you can count. Yes, you can.*

17. **Do not cut the umbilical cord.** *Put the scissors down!*

18. **Check kittens for choking/gurgling sounds.** *Breathe, breathe, breathe. Almost there!*
19. **Make sure each kitten nurses.**

The above list is actually a *greatly* edited and simplified version of the real instructions offered to cat owners participating in a birth event.

So you can follow all of the above steps, or you can try Method B:

1. **Do absolutely nothing.***

Both methods will produce exactly the same results: a healthy litter of kittens. Actually, that is not true. Method B will statistically lead to a healthier mother and litter of kittens because it will not entail you nervously dropping the kittens; you stepping on mom's nest in your

frantic haste to find her a safe place to nest; or you pulling, scrubbing, pinching, snipping, or cauterizing things that should not be pulled, scrubbed, pinched, snipped, or cauterized.

But still, a dedicated Catakist cannot be persuaded to take a hands-off approach to something as mind-bendingly miraculous as the arrival of a litter of kittens. She is psychologically compelled to take a management position, so as to make herself indispensable to her cat (at least in her own mind).

*not actually possible for a Catakist.

XI. The Blessed Day

When thinking about the high points of our lives, most of us remember our first kiss, our college graduation, *American Idol's* inaugural season, or even our wedding day. All of those things are *nice*, but for a Catakist, the day that remains etched in memory, even when she can no longer remember her own name, is the day(s) her cat had kittens.

Kitten Birth Day is an event ideally accompanied by champagne, cakes, gifts, live music, confetti, and, if the budget allows, parades with marching bands. It is the culmination of a long process that includes painting and decorating the kitten nursery, buying kitten clothes and toys, designing and printing the birth announcements, and purchasing the extra batteries and memory cards for the camera.

The biggest shock the Catakist faces at birth time is realizing that her job does not allow a paid leave of absence for kitten care (note to self: when the rush is over, start a petition for paid cat maternity leave). This creates an enormous problem, because for the next six weeks, the Catakist puts her entire life on hold. She does not work, she does not cook, she does not clean, she does not shower or feed herself. No. She *helps* with the kittens morning, noon, and night.

Much to the dismay of the mother cat.

XII. Angels Descend to Earth

In Catakism, the arrival of the kittens is nothing short of an angelic visitation. Normal life ceases, and a period of intense religious service begins.

The first thing the human does when kittens are born is announce to the human family: "We must not name the kittens, because that will only make it harder to part with them when it's time to find them new homes."

The second thing the human does is name the kittens.

The third thing the human does is fall madly in love with each and every one of the furry cuties.

The fourth thing the human does is announce that virtually no human home on Earth will be good enough to merit receiving one of the sacred kittens.

With permanent residence of all the kittens thus firmly established, the human's anxiety level goes down and she can go about the business of turning her life over to kitten servitude.

Kitten-proofing the home. When kittens arrive, the first practical step the human family must take is to kitten-proof the home. That means removing everything a kitten can:

- swallow
- knock over
- chew on
- break
- fall into
- pee on
- spill
- hide in
- turn on
- play with
- climb

In short, that means removing everything from the house except the litter box and food and water dishes. This is not a problem for devoted Catakists, who no longer *want* to do anything but play with the kittens, video the kittens, cuddle the kittens, and turn the entire home into a kitten playpen.

Fretting over feeding and care. During the first several weeks of life, the kittens get all of their nourishment from their mom. It is the mother cat's job to feed and care for the kittens. It is the human's job to hover over mom 24/7 and fret about it. This eventually stresses the mom cat out so much that her milk dries up and she starts ignoring her kittens and staring into space with slightly folded ears. At this point, the human deems it necessary to take over the care and feeding of the kittens, which is what she was secretly angling for all along.

Weaning the kittens. When it's time for the kittens to transition to solid food, the human begins to have more frets than a double-neck electric guitar. For it becomes the human's job, not the mother cat's, to oversee the weaning process. At this point, the human no longer sleeps at night, due to absolute certainty that the kittens are going to die of starvation before dawn.

The human starts the weaning process by making a soggy mash of dairy product and dry cat food. If the kittens eat this, the human enters a state of profound euphoria. If the kittens do not eat, she calls 911 ten times a day.

Eventually, of course, the kittens transition to "regular" food, because that's what kittens do, and the human is so proud of her animal husbandry skills, she awards herself the Albert Schweitzer Gold Medal for Humanitarianism and quits her job to become a frontier veterinarian.

Finding new homes. Eventually—unless she is a certified crazy cat lady—the human will realize that she cannot, in fact, keep all the kittens. Not if she wishes to keep her job, her mind, her security deposit, and, oh yeah, her spouse (if one is deemed necessary). At this point, the screening and interview process for adoptive parents begins.

Writing the questionnaire. The first step in this process is to create a set of questions to ask all potential adopters. These range from the basics, such as religion (i.e., Catakism), income level, and political beliefs, to more complex concerns, such as foreign entanglements, recent visits to regions where certain fungal infections are common, and diversification of stock portfolio.

Placing the ad. In bygone eras, when one wanted to place kittens, one wrote "Free Kittens" on the back of a beer carton and nailed it to one's garage. Today, putting kittens up for adoption involves a long-range social media campaign. It begins by chumming the waters with strategically placed online photos of the kittens in pom-pom hats. Later it evolves into a sophisticated marketing strategy that creates a sense of exclusivity.

Interviewing the applicants. Assuming all of the candidates have been given a thorough background check, filled out their questionnaires, and had their names googled for any potentially anti-feline remarks made in the past, it's time to move ahead with the interview process.

There is no set formula for the adoption interview, except that it should be grueling, long, offensive, and intrusive, so as to drive away any but the most dedicated and committed humans. The most important part of the interview, of course, is the meeting of the kittens. If one of the kittens *chooses* the human by purring, kneading, rubbing against, or giving the soft eyes, the deal is sealed.

The kitten always has the last word, and its word is sacred.

Bow to the Meow.

PURR-MINOLOGY

Cat Glory and Exaltation Day—A special holiday in the Catakism calendar set aside for the praise and adoration of cats. Celebrated three hundred sixty-five days per year.

Cat Mitzvah—A sacred ritual in which a fledgling believer adopts Catakism as his or her lifelong faith.

Cat Park—The Internet.

Cat-a-gorical Imperative—The requirement, in Catakism, that cats be regarded as simultaneously dignified and noble, cute and cuddly, and insanely funny.

Catakism—The formal practice of devoting one's life to the praise, adoration, and service of cats.

Catakist—A practitioner of Catakism.

Cat-a-littic Conversion—The precise moment in time—usually accompanied by intense purring in one's lap—when one converts to Catakism.

Cat-astrophe—A tragedy of feline proportions.

Catatonic Navigational Disorder—The tendency to allow your subconscious to take over while driving and find yourself parked outside a cat shelter, cat show, or pet store and having no idea how you got there. However, upon arrival, you think to yourself, "Now that I'm here, I might as well go check out the kitty cats."

Catma—The (ahem) dogma of Catakism.

Cattict—One who is addicted to cats.

Cattitude—The exquisite blend of superiority, coolness, sleekness, aloofness, confidence, mystery, smarts, and unpredictability exuded by cats, which compels humans to bow down before them and feed them flaked filet of sole in crystal chalices.

CEO—Cat Executive Officer, i.e., the head of your household.

Chatachisme—Catakism *en français.*

Coming Out of the Claws-et—Publicly declaring one's devotion to Cat.

Crazy Cat Lady—What all Catakists, regardless of gender, become when they begin *hosting* three or more cats in their homes.

Dogtology—The (heretical) belief in dogs as more worship-worthy than cats.

DICK (Doesn't Idolize Cats or Kittens)—A human who just didn't get the meow-mo.

Eternal Sin Against Cat—An unforgivable transgression against a kitty, such as moving a sleeping cat, laughing at a cat, startling a cat, et *catera.*

Ex-claw-munication—The revocation of one's Catakism membership due to demonstrated unworthiness (e.g., committing an Eternal Sin Against Cat; see above).

Feline Deprivation Disorder—The constellation of physical and psychological symptoms a Catakist suffers when going more than an hour without seeing, petting, and/or holding a cat.

Feline Falsetto Frequency (FFF or Triple-F)—The high-pitched, servile, baby talk tone of voice all humans are compelled to use when conversing with a cat.

Feline Mind Meld—The state of hypnosis a cat puts a human under by using a strategic combination of slow blinks, purrs, and "the soft eyes."

Feline Numerical Dysfunction—A disorder experienced by advanced-level Catakists in which the sufferer loses the ability to accurately report how many cats she has in her home (perhaps for fear of being labeled a crazy cat lady).

Glare of Damnation—The disapproving look a cat gives to let you know you have committed an Eternal Sin Against Cat (see above).

Kitten Smitten—An early stage of Catakism in which one's feline devotion is focused almost exclusively on kittens (kittens are the gateway drug to cat obsession).

Litteral—Related to, or having to do with litter boxes *or* litters of kittens.

Nine Sacred Attributes of Cat—The special qualities and powers cats possess, such as the ability to teleport, liquefy, and do the Feline Mind Meld (see above), which render felines worthy of human adulation.

Ninefold Path—The guidelines of spiritual faith laid down in time immemorial for all practicing Catakists to follow.

Posterior Power Play—The historical moment (in the mid-twentieth century) when cats began allowing humans to assume full responsibility for their poops, thus cementing humans as permanently lower on the totem pole than kitties.

Power of the Pussycat—Cats have it. It's the Catakist version of Kryptonite. No further explanation required.

Psy-cat-ic—The mental state of Catakists.

Purr-aphernalia—The assortment of *religious* artifacts (e.g., cat toys, cat posters, cat knickknacks, cat furniture, cat-themed mugs and T-shirts) that turn a human home into a Temple of Catakism.

Purr-formance Art—Any song-and-dance number performed by a human for the exclusive "enjoyment" of their cat.

Sacred Purr—A cat's meditative mantra, which she chants constantly in order to stay spiritually centered in the presence of humans.

Urine Nasal Blindness—A disorder in which longtime "host families" to cats lose the ability to notice the odor of cat urine pervading their household.

YouTubular Compulsivity—The addictive need to watch cat videos 24/7.

ACKNOWLEDGMENTS

This catma would not be possible without the endless love and support from D.E. and the always giving friendship from A.W.

Thank you to cats everywhere for reminding me who the boss really is . . . and for being so stinkin' cute!

To all the cats I have personally known in my life: thank you for not killing me and for showing me that cats are people too.

MY CAT-A-LITTIC CONVERSION

About the Author

I grew up in a dog house. Not an actual doghouse; I mean we were dog people. Cats were these mysterious creatures that lived with *other* people, not us. I was never a DICK, mind you. I was always *interested* in cats. But, frankly, I wasn't totally sure what all the fuss was about. For one thing, I noticed that every cat house (ahem) I entered had this "piquant" odor, and I found it just a bit appalling that people could live with open boxes of poop on their floors. Then there was the fact that the moment I stepped into a cat house, I would develop the same symptoms as a full-blown cold.

Bottom line: I had a certain coolness about approaching cats. Oh, I always *tried* to make kitty contact, but sensing my hestitance, cats would keep their distance from me. I'd feel a bit rejected, but I learned to live with that.

Then one day, the Power of the Pussycat brought me in from exile. I walked into a friend's house, and a cat came scurrying up to me with an excited chirp. It began purring and weaving around my legs. My heart wanted to burst—I was being honored by a cat's affections. Suddenly, I *got* it. I knew what all the fuss was about. And I noticed something remarkable—my allergy was gone! But more than that: I had been *accepted* into the Litter of the Faithful. Salvation was mine at last! I'd had my Cat-a-littic Conversion! Now I, too, could put Persians on pedestals and pay homage to Himalayans!

These days, when I enter a house *without* a cat, I ask, "What's that *weird* odor?"